Maud Wilder Goodwin

White Aprons, a Romance of Bacon's Rebellion

Virginia, 1676

Maud Wilder Goodwin

White Aprons, a Romance of Bacon's Rebellion
Virginia, 1676

ISBN/EAN: 9783743308923

Manufactured in Europe, USA, Canada, Australia, Japa

Cover: Foto ©ninafisch / pixelio.de

Manufactured and distributed by brebook publishing software
(www.brebook.com)

Maud Wilder Goodwin

White Aprons, a Romance of Bacon's Rebellion

CONTENTS.

		PAGE
I.	Penelope	11
II.	In Camp	28
III.	Flag of Truce	51
IV.	Hearts of Gold	71
V.	A Trader	88
VI.	Montague and Capulet	103
VII.	The King's Commission	117
VIII.	Laodiceans	138
IX.	The Valley of the Shadow	155
X.	Vengeance	164
XI.	The Trial of Bryan Fairfax	178
XII.	Penelope's Pilgrimage	212
XIII.	Over Seas	224
XIV.	The Lions of London	238
XV.	Three Letters	254
XVI.	Penelope goes to Court	268
XVII.	A Private Interview	287
XVIII.	A Foy	301
XIX.	April Twenty-third	320

WHITE APRONS.

CHAPTER I.

PENELOPE.

"Hath she her faults? I would you had them too:
They are the fruity must of soundest wine."

ROSEMARY HALL stood four-square at the head of a winding creek which flows into the York River. It was counted in its day the finest mansion in tide-water Virginia. Its posts and beams were hewn from the giant pines of the primeval forest, and were of a size and thickness to put our modern cardboard frames to shame.

There was something of nobleness in the very plainness of the house. Its square outlines and broad sweep of roof were marked by a simple dignity which fitly comported with the lives led within the shelter of its walls. Perchance to one familiar with the stately stone mansions of the old world the term "Hall" might have sounded over-ambitious for this plain house of wood; but those who knew Colonel Theophilus Payne, its owner, realized that pretension of any kind was foreign to his nature. It was rather his very simplicity which led him to cling to all the traditions of the old home, and still, after a quarter of a century, to cherish the name hallowed by early associations.

Nor was its name all that Rosemary Hall had borrowed from England. Everything within its walls gave hint of having come hither from a land across the seas, — the carved oaken cupboard in the corner of the dining-room, the pewter and silver plate which shone on its shelves, the fire-dogs on the hearth, the high-backed chairs in the wide saloon, the slender-legged spinet which was the Hall's chief ornament, — nay, not the chief, for that was the maiden who sat before the spinet, this September afternoon, surrounded by the slant glory of the autumn sun, which touched her red-brown hair to the color of burnished copper, and played about the curves of her rounded throat.

To attempt the portrait of beauty is ever a difficult task for brush or pen, since beauty is a harmony which fixes itself less in the mind than discord. Moreover, it is so cheap a dowry that few romancers have been able to resist bestowing it upon their heroines; and it has become so common that the reader turns away sated from the inventory of charms, and well-nigh longs for a wart on the nose, or some break in the monotonous category of perfections.

It is not without hesitation, therefore, that I set down the fact forced upon me by the cumulative testimony of tradition, and of an old portrait still existing, that Penelope Payne was beautiful. Yet in extenuation of the statement be it said, that her beauty was a harmonious discord and her face was full of faults. Her nose was too short, and bore a tiny row of freckles along its bridge. Her mouth was too wide, and its upper lip too sharply curved. Her coloring suggested the old saying, —

> "Hair and eyes that match in hue
> Mark the sibyl or the shrew."

In this case the proverb bade fair to be doubly true, for a quick brain, a warm heart, and a hot temper were so blended that none could say which in the end would conquer and take the lead. This was a question to be settled in large measure by the influences under which her life might chance to fall hereafter.

The girl's dress was marked by that sobriety which in colonial regions subdued the coquetry of a costume devised to meet the tastes of the fair and free dames of the court of the second Charles. Her shoes were of russet leather, and the suspicion of hose which showed above them was of the same hue. The gown was of flowered dimity, looped back to show a sad-colored paragon petticoat, and over this fell an apron of some soft white stuff. The bodice was cut low, but the shoulders above it hid themselves modestly beneath a snowy white whisk whose ruffled ends were demurely crossed and snugly secured at the waist. Only the arms were left bare, and showed their supple curves and dimpled elbows as the maiden's fingers wandered idly over the wooden keys of the old spinet. The music-book before her fluttered its leaves so vexingly in the breeze that the girl moved with a little exclamation of impatience to close the door of the saloon, which stood always open as though in token of the ever ready welcome which Rosemary offered to all comers. As she rose from the spinet, one could see that the maid's height was above the common. Long of limb was she, with the lithe, far-reaching stride of some wild thing of the forest who had never learned the mincing gait of the civilized world.

It seemed a pity thus to shut out the jocund sunlight which had played so merrily through the room; but the music fluttered no more, and the girl turned the leaves at her leisure as she tried the sweet old tunes. In her clear, youthful, unimpassioned voice she sang of the loves of Corydon and Phyllis, of the faithful affection of Prettye Bessie, of Barbara Allen's cruelty, and of the shrouded lover who once went in cockle hat and sandal shoon.

"Ah," cried she at last, "I have found it. Beshrew me if I do not learn it against my father's home-coming, for he doth much affect it. Hearken," she said, shaking her finger playfully at the white dove which had flown in from the porch as she closed the door and now sat perched upon her shoulder, — "hearken and peck me if I do not sing it straight.

"'Over the mountains and over the waves,
  Under the fountains and under the graves,
  Under floods that are deepest which Neptune obey,
  Over rocks that are steepest, Love will find out the way.'"

"*Thump! Thump! Thump!*"

The wrought-iron knocker on the closed door broke in rudely upon the sweet strains of the song as it thundered its announcement of a visitor, and a visitor in haste. The sudden noise sent the white dove fluttering up among the beams of the timbered ceiling, and brought the maiden to her feet.

"Pomp, where are you? Some one waits at the door."

Silence reigned in answer to the call of the young voice; and as the heavy ring fell again upon the unfeeling breast of the iron lion, the door was flung back, and Penelope Payne stood in the doorway framed in like a picture with a background of panelled wall. Like some stately goddess she seemed to the eyes of the stranger, and a not too friendly divinity either, if one might judge from the curling lip and the disdainful eye which fell on the green cockade in the hat of the young man before her, — a badge which marked him as an officer in Bacon's troops.

"I crave your pardon for the abruptness of my summons," said the soldier, sweeping the floor of the porch with the plumes of his hat, "but may I ask if Mistress Payne be at home?"

"I trust I impeach not the hospitality of our house when I make answer that my mother is never at home to rebels."

Straight and tall and white she stood as she flung him back this answer. Only an angry spot of red showed in either cheek, and the eyes that had been soft and tender grew dark and stormy.

"I grieve the more over your inhospitable mood that I find myself compelled to intrude without your permission, since I am ordered by General Bacon to find Mistress Payne and bring her with all despatch to his camp at Green Spring, where she will find Madam Ballard and other neighbors awaiting her arrival. I was ordered to fetch Mistress Wormley also, but I found her too ill to leave her home."

The girl's lip curled more than before as she answered: "'T is like your brave general to wage war against women. Knowing that my father was gone to join Governor Berkeley at Jamestown, he felt sure of finding us defenceless. Methinks, under the circumstances, one gallant officer might have sufficed to do his errand; but I see you have brought four men with ye, to be your guard against two women."

The young man flushed and would have spoken; but ere he could find words, the girl continued: "I pray you of your courtesy to make known to us for what purpose our presence is desired by General Bacon. Hath he sent for us to teach him manners, the which, if what is said of him be true, he hath great need to learn?"

"I fear I must consent to share that lack of courtesy you do impute to him when I reply that it was not your presence, but that of your mother, which I am ordered to secure, and that I am commanded to give no whys or wherefores."

"How now, Penelope! Who is this you keep standing thus without? Was ever guest permitted to tarry on the porch of Rosemary Hall, unwelcomed to all within?"

As she spoke these words, the lady whom Major Fairfax had come to seek appeared in the doorway. He felt of a sudden ashamed of his errand, as he saw the placid motherly face beaming with friendly welcome, and the gentle little hand held out heartily to the stranger. The eyesight of Madam Payne, less keen than that of her daughter, saw in the young man before her only a traveller, come, after the good old fashion of Virginia, to seek a night's shelter. Her daughter made answer bitterly: "This is no guest, mother, but an enemy, come in the name of Nathaniel Bacon to take us prisoners, and bring us to his general."

"Nay, not you," interrupted the officer.

"I go with my mother," quoth the young goddess, looming taller and grander than ever.

"So be it," replied Fairfax, shrugging his shoulders. "Such be not my orders, but I will not say you 'nay;' only I pray you make haste, for we must be at Green Spring ere nightfall."

"Penelope," said Madam Payne, with a wonderful dignity and serenity, "let us not wonder that this rebel general, who respects not lawful authority, should respect no more the claims of womanhood. Let us go, since go we must, with a courage which shall not put your father's name to shame. Prithee, sir," she added, turning toward Fairfax, "lead on; we await your commands."

"I do assure you, Madam Payne, it grieves me more to command than it can you to obey. As for what I spake of haste just now 't was not to be pushed so far. I can readily grant you time for the donning of cloak and hood and safeguard."

"Not so," said the girl, with the petulance of youth, which next to its own way most ardently cherishes a love of martyrdom. "Since we ride not of our free will, we will make no preparations. Ye must needs take us as we are."

"Come, then, my daughter," said her mother, passing her arm through that of Penelope, "let us tarry no longer, for the day is far spent, and we must not put this gentleman to inconvenience."

Fairfax looked swiftly at her, suspicious of irony; but her face was calm and undisturbed. She and her daughter moved slowly down the garden path between the low hedges. As they passed a bed of rosemary, Penelope paused, and stooping, plucked a scarlet cluster, which she thrust into the bosom of her dress. A single tear fell upon it. "Alas," said she to her mother, "'t is all of Rosemary that we can carry with us."

"Nay, my daughter, for we may take also that faith and fortitude which have builded Rosemary thus, as 't were in the wilderness, and which are our best stay in these troublous times."

The fusileers presented arms in token of respect as the women passed them; but one being over slow, the Major struck him with the flat of his sword. "Next time," cried he angrily, "know enough to show respect for your betters, all the more when they are in misfortune, and especially to these ladies whom General Bacon hath commanded to be treated with all consideration."

At the gate which opened upon the highroad, two led horses, one of which had been designed for Mistress Wormley, were in waiting, and on these the ladies were mounted, disdaining any help save from their own servants, who had followed them to the gate in a sorrowful procession.

"Pompey," said Madam Payne to the gray-haired negro who stood at her stirrup, "I charge you keep all here in my absence as safe as the lawlessness around us doth permit. Listen, Hannibal, and you, Polly, and all the rest: I have put all matters into the hands of Pompey, and you are to obey him faithfully."

"Yes, Missus."

"De Lawd hab mercy."

"What am a-gwine ter happen?"

Amid such wails as these the procession moved away from the gates of Rosemary, Penelope ever and anon turning back for one more look at the dear old house standing solitary and deserted in the slant light of the afternoon sun.

To outward eye it was a gay little cavalcade that moved forward along the sandy road under the fragrant pine-trees this soft summer day; for the outward eye takes no note of hatred and bitterness and all the seething passions that disturb the soul. All that a bystander would have observed was a couple of ladies out for a ride with their escort, which the warlike time no doubt made necessary.

In front rode two of the fusileers, their weapons clanking against their saddles. Next came the dame and damsel in their singular riding-dress of lawn and lace and flowered chintz. This strange attire might have caused a smile in one given to seeing the comic side of life, as Fairfax had ever been; but now, as he rode behind them, he felt only a sense of inward confusion and vexation.

"'Sdeath," said he to himself, "I would our general had commissioned Lawrence, or Drummond, or any but me on this errand. A war with women hath naught of credit in it. If they conquer, a man is a fool; if he conquer, he is a brute, or feeleth himself such, as I do now."

"Here, you," he called to one of the men riding in the rear, "dismount and pluck me off that bough of alder yonder by the brook, — yea, that one which hath the thickest covering of leaves. Now strip off the knots and roughness of the stem,— so; 't is well."

When he had two boughs prepared thus to his liking, he called aloud to those in front to come to a halt. All four horses stood still. The fusileers looked back, but the women deigned not to turn their heads. Leaping from his horse, Fairfax walked forward, and, stepping between the ladies, proffered each a bough, that their eyes might be shielded from the rays of the western sun which fell full in their faces as they journeyed.

The girl tossed her branch contemptuously into the dust, saying as she did so, "I accept neither shade nor shelter from the hand of a traitor."

But her mother chid her, saying: "Thou art

wrong, my daughter. Remember the conduct of the martyred king, who recognized every, even the least, courtesy, though 't was offered him at the foot of the scaffold, considering what was due to himself rather than what was due to his enemies. I thank you, sir," she added, turning toward Fairfax; and thenceforward she rode beneath the green shade of the alder bough.

After this they went on in silence, save for such sound as the song of the birds in the trees, or the crackle of breaking branches when some startled animal scurried into hiding. Major Fairfax rode with slackened bridle a dozen paces behind the women folk, looking now at the head beneath the green shade, then at the rebellious one beside it crowned with red-brown hair which fell in soft curls about the shoulders. Of the face Fairfax could gain no glimpse; for it never turned itself by so much as an inch to right or left. At length, for lack of better companionship, Fairfax bent over the neck of his mare, and fell to talking softly in her ear, — a trick he had learned through riding alone, boy and man, in the forest at home. The huntsman were solitary indeed if he did not make friends of his horse and his dog.

"I tell ye, Peggy," quoth her rider, "you females are strange beings. You will sacrifice the real thing for the show, all of you. Yes, Peggy, 'tis vain to shake your head. 'T is true, ye jade, and you know it. Why, I have seen you go shying and curveting past a brushwood fire by the roadside, quite content to pass, if only you could make your rider uneasy lest he find himself on his back in the road. 'T is even so with women. Now perchance you, being of the same sex, can tell me why yonder haughty minx must needs make herself so unpleasant in the doing of that which she knows must be done. Had she been a man that met my courtesy after such unhandsome fashion, I would have run her through with my sword; but because she is a woman forsooth, I must pocket the affront and be cap in hand to her Highness. I swear, Peggy, 'tis passing hard. Were it not for her mother I would give myself scant pains to be civil; but for Madam Payne, she hath not only disarmed me, but armed me in her service."

Near in body but far apart in soul, the riders moved along thus, each busy with his own thoughts and recking little of those of the others. The sun was already set and the shades of evening were deepening when at length they drew rein before the gates of Green Spring. Here they were stopped by a cry of "Halt!" and the question, "Who goes there?"

"Friends," answered Fairfax.

"Advance, and give the countersign," said the voice from the darkness.

"Right and our rights."

"Pass on," said the sentry, as he swung the gate open.

The horses, worn with their long journey through the heat, stumbled slowly up the winding road. Madam Payne thought sadly of the first time she had ridden beneath those trees, — the evening of the ball given by the Governor in honor of the restoration of King Charles II. to the throne of England. But what a change had come over Green Spring since that joyful night! Then every window was ablaze with candles, and lanterns twinkled from every tree. Now the woods were as dark as the times, and not a light glimmered from the close-barred windows. Not one, did I say? Yes, a single lamp gave a feeble brightness to the porch, and by its light Madam Payne could see a man standing on the steps to receive them. It needed not the lace upon his coat to proclaim him a man of rank. The women knew at once that they were in the presence of the rebel general, Nathaniel Bacon.

"'Thou art late with thine escort, Fairfax. Hanford is already come with Dame Ballard and Dame

Bray. Hadst thou tarried much longer I must needs have sent in search of thee, fearing thou hadst been captured by the enemy or fallen into some ambush of Berkeley's."

"Sir William Berkeley," said a woman's voice from the darkness, "fights not in ambush but on the open field, and being himself a gentleman, he could not dream that defenceless women were being torn from their homes and stood in need of his protection."

At the first words General Bacon turned his head, and peered from beneath his hand into the night. At the word *gentleman* he started as if stung, then commanded himself, and, vouchsafing no answer, addressed himself once more to Fairfax.

"Major Fairfax, you will take these ladies to the dining-room, where supper is awaiting them, and where they will find their friends already arrived."

The horses moved up to the block, and Fairfax assisted Madam Payne to alight; but when he turned to give his hand to her daughter, she had slipped from the saddle and passed up the steps, vouchsafing neither word nor glance. At the top she paused, her slender form and delicate profile outlined against the light in the hallway. General Bacon studied her closely as she stood thus.

"A plague on Fairfax!" he muttered. "Why did he bring this shrewish beauty to pester us,—and without orders too? 'T is the daughter of Mistress Payne belike. What was that she said? '*He being himself a gentleman*—' Bah! none can fight battles with roses, nor run governments by the golden rule; no, nor play the gentleman in a matter of strategy of war. Yet I would it had not been necessary."

Turning on his heel, he found Fairfax again at his side, and thrusting his arm into the breast of his coat he drew out a paper, which he placed in the young officer's hand. "'T is your orders for to-morrow, Major," he said; "study them well, and fail not by jot or tittle in their fulfilment." With this he turned and entered the house with heavy and slow step, while the bugle sounded retreat and night fell on the rebel camp. As Fairfax came out of the doorway on his way to his tent, he saw lying on the floor of the porch a little faded, shrivelled bit of rosemary. He did not pick it up, but he put it gently one side with his foot. He could not quite tread on it.

CHAPTER II.

IN CAMP.

> " The hum of either army stilly sounds
> That the fixed sentinels almost receive
> The secret whispers of each other's watch;
> Fire answers fire, and through their paly flames
> Each battle sees the other's umbered face."

IT was the hour before dawn, — the dreariest hour of the twenty-four, the period when the vitality of the world is at its lowest ebb, when the clock in the sick-room ticks slowest, when the night-lamp flickers before expiring, and the pulse of the sufferer likewise flickers, and perchance goes out, before day rises with its fresh tide of life and vigor.

Everything about the plantation of Green Spring this morning shared the tone of melancholy and depression. The ghastly sound of spades grating against fresh earth, and of dirt falling in heavy thuds, suggested the making of a grave. The constant hammering was as the driving of nails in a coffin or the rearing of a scaffold. Here and

In Camp.

there lanterns flitted to and fro, and voices, sounding weird and strange, called to each other across the open trench. But at length, in contrast to their dimness, a quick, decided tone was heard uttering orders sharp and clear.

"Throw up the breastworks higher on the side of the James City road! Mount another gun and train it on the river! You fools! waste no more time upon that ditch at your backs. 'T is not the red men from the forest, but the whites from the town, that we must fortify against."

As the eye of the master is a spur in the side of the servant, so is the presence of the leader to the soldier. At the sound of Bacon's voice the labor was redoubled. The men worked like beavers in early spring. Swiftly as the general made his rounds, his quick eye took note of every shovel and every man holding it.

"Perry, you look ill. Throw down that spade and get you to bed. Any one can dig, but few can fight like you; and we shall have need of all our good fighters ere this day be out."

"West, I need not oversee the setting of your gun. Whate'er you do is well done. I would I had a regiment of such."

Words like these cost little, but they count for much. "I tell thee," said Perry to West as Bacon moved on, "'t is not every leader who doth thus consider the private soldier."

"Nay, verily," answered West; "but he do look upon us as so bound up with him that our good or ill is in truth his own."

"Ay, we must all make common cause else are we lost, and that speedily. But lost or saved, I for one grieve not that we have taken up arms. Methinks we stood still too long, seeing our crops stolen and our houses burned by those marauding Indians, and all because of this rusty, crusty old Governor, who has cheated the grave-digger when he should have been under ground these ten years. Because this dotard sees fit to refuse us permission to fight, shall we submit? Faith, 't is asking too much of human nature. We were worse than cowards did we flinch, most of all when heaven sends such a man as Nathaniel Bacon to lead us."

"Ay, he was born with a lucky star; and be we but faithful, it shall shine on our fortunes as well."

Meanwhile, Bacon himself was walking on, reflecting with no such cheerful assurance on the future. Thus far, to be sure, all had gone well beyond his hopes, until now the strange chances of war had fixed his headquarters here at Green Spring, Sir William Berkeley's plantation, which on this September morning, in the year sixteen hundred and seventy-six, he was strengthening with earthworks and fortifying with guns, to receive the expected visit from its owner. So far, well; but who should say what this day now dawning might bring forth? Berkeley was encamped at Jamestown, only four miles away, with a force which outnumbered his three to one, and it was an open secret that the Governor intended to attack this very morning.

"Time," muttered Bacon, talking to himself as he walked, according to his wont, — "time is all I ask. Were Berkeley shrewd enough to make a night attack, as I would have done in his place, our game were up; but my spy says the attack is planned for seven o' the clock. 'T is too early for my taste. Let my earthworks but be finished and my guns set, I will promise them a welcome shall send them back howling like whipped curs to Jamestown. But we cannot hope to have all in readiness till high noon. What then? Why, the fox's craft must eke out the lion's courage. Yet I own I like it not. It savors too much of Lawrence's subtlety; and then, should aught befall these women, not even the success of our cause could console me. I swear I like it not."

With this Bacon began gnawing at his mustachio (a sure sign of vexation of spirit in him), and stood still, a heavy frown gathering on his brow, till of a sudden he caught sight of Fairfax marching toward the stables, swinging his lantern and trolling as he strode along in gay, careless soldier fashion: —

> "Jog on, jog on the footpath way,
> And merrily hent the stile-a.
> Your merry heart goes all the day,
> Your sad tires in a mile-a."

"Bless the lad!" cried Bacon, a smile breaking over his gloom, "'t is not the first time he hath cheered me. The sunshine of his nature hath somewhat of contagion in 't. Moreover he is the trustiest man in all my following, and of a truth there is no other to whom I would have committed the delicate business of the care of these women."

It was with a lighter heart that he continued his walk, and finally mounted the steps of the mansion and flung open the door of the dining-room, where his officers were assembled in council of war and impatiently awaiting his coming. The table around which they sat was of oak, heavily carved and black with age. For well-nigh thirty years it had faithfully served Sir William Berkeley. It had held up his viands, and sometimes his guests, when the good Madeira and Fayal, which ever flowed bountifully at Green Spring, had mounted to the gentlemen's heads. This same table had borne patiently many a resounding blow from Sir William's fist, when after dinner he had called his friends to order and cried out: "Now, gentlemen, one last toast, and we will, if you please, drink it standing — 'God save His Majesty King Charles!'"

If wood can feel (and who shall say otherwise?) this stanch loyalist table must have trembled with wrath to feel itself now surrounded by rebels planning war against its owner, — and indeed it did seem to creak, as if in an agony of apprehension, when General Bacon, striding abruptly into the room, unbuckled his sword and threw it clanking down upon the table, and at the same time rapped heavily upon its carven edge.

"Well, gentlemen," said he, peering through the half light at the tall Dutch clock in the corner, "it wants but three hours of seven o'clock, — the hour when the spy (and I think he is trustworthy) informs me Lord Berkeley has planned his attack. We have time, but none to waste. Fairfax," he added, turning to the young man who stood in the doorway about to enter, "are the horses saddled?"

"Yes, General."

"And the lady called?"

"No, for you named her not."

"True — true — I did put off the decision — plague on my vacillation! Let me see, which shall it be? Which *shall* it be? Not Dame Ballard, for her tongue is too blunt; not my kinswoman Dame Bacon, for her temper is too sharp. Not Madam Payne, for she is too fine a woman to suffer aught of discourtesy which can be avoided. I have it. It shall be her daughter.

"Major Fairfax, call Mistress Penelope Payne (so I think she is named); and that her mother may endure no apprehension on her behalf, inform Madam Payne that her daughter is to be sent with an escort to James City, bearing a message to her father and Governor Berkeley."

The young officer bowed and withdrew. Sooth to say he liked his errand little, and the more he thought of it the less he liked it. More reluctantly than he would have approached a frowning fortress did he mount the winding stairs, and draw near the chamber door, before which a sentry, stiff and still as a wooden soldier, was keeping guard.

Fairfax rapped sharply against the panel, and as the echo fell upon his ear, it recalled the indignant apparition which his knock at the door of Rosemary Hall had called up, and he would rather have faced Berkeley's batteries than this young fury. But a true hero will not flinch, even before a woman; and Fairfax stood his ground.

His rapping roused the five women within the chamber. In fact, they needed little rousing, for their slumbers had been brief and fitful. Most of them reclined on arm-chairs and couches, with which the luxurious taste of Lady Berkeley had supplied the room. Mistress Ballard, however, whose hair-dressing was the admiration of the colony, — a miracle of taste, labor, and ingenuity, — unwilling to risk its destruction, was sitting bolt upright in a stiff, high-backed chair, the cherished locks carefully supported by its cross-bar.

"What is wanted?" she called aloud in answer to the summons.

"I must beg of you to open the door at your earliest convenience," said the voice of Fairfax outside. "I must see you, that I may the better explain my errand. General Bacon desires the attendance of one of your number in the dining-room below, where he and his officers be now assembled."

"Good Lord!" cried Madam Ballard, "I hope it's not me that's wanted. I am such a fright before breakfast! I was in such a flutter when they fetched me from the plantation that I bethought me not to take with me my powder puff, nor my rouge ball, nor even my eye-brow stick; and there was my cramoisie stomacher lying new in my drawer and I never fetched it. Not that it matters; but one would not wish to appear before gentlemen, rebels though they be, in such a plight. 'T is one thing not to think well of men, but 't is quite another not to wish them to think well of me."

"Ha, my lady," thought Fairfax, "I have your gauge; but methinks you are likely this day to forget even your vanity."

"Sure the summons cannot be for me," said the voice of Dame Bray, who scarce bestirred herself to turn toward the door, but lay yawning and spreading her much-ringed fingers before her sleepy eyes. "Master Bacon has visited in my house, and he knows I never rise before noon. Why, I would not have a negar called at this hour."

"I only hope I am the one," snapped little Madam Bacon. "I crave naught more than the chance to speak my mind to Nat." The spiteful sparkle in the lady's eyes and the tightening of her thin lips indicated that the piece of her mind which she contemplated bestowing on her kinsman would be more blessed to give than to receive.

"I have often told my husband," she continued,

speaking high and shrill, " that he was nourishing a viper in his bosom; and now when this treacherous villain has put me to death, I shall have the comfort of knowing what I said hath come true. Ladies," she added solemnly, " if any of you should chance to survive me, I would have you see to it that 'I told you so' is inscribed upon my gravestone."

The handle of the chamber door was shaken impatiently. " I prithee, ladies, make greater haste, for I must enter, and that speedily. Time is precious, and I can waste no more. Besides, you are throwing away your words; for it is none of you who are wanted below, but Mistress Penelope Payne."

" At your service," cried that young woman, flinging the door wide, though her mother clung to her, saying over and over in tones pathetically tremulous, " Oh, no — not her — not her — I pray you, sir, take *me*."

" Madam Payne," said Fairfax, entering, and bowing low to each lady in turn, but lowest and with most reverence to her whom he addressed, "suffer not the least apprehension. General Bacon is, as you all know, and in spite of all ill spoke against him, a man of his word, and he bids me assure you that your daughter shall come to no harm. He doth but intend to send her under safe escort to James City, bearing a message to Governor Berkeley, to which — so at least our General thinks — he will pay the more heed that it comes from one of his own party."

At these words the older woman relaxed her eager clasp, though the anxiety cleared not altogether from her brow. Penelope, with that lightness of heart with which youth doth ever enter on untried adventure, turned from one to the other of her companions and cried almost mirthfully: " Fare ye well, friends, though I trust but for a time. I will bear in mind all ye have said when I am yonder at James City. Madam Ballard, I will strive to supply the necessaries of your toilet if I have luck to find them, that you may not change color in the face of danger. Madam Bray, I will report having seen you as none ever did before, — awake ere dawn. Mistress Bacon, I will assure your husband on your own authority that he hath cherished a viper in his bosom. For you, Madam Mother, since you never crave aught for yourself, I know not what I can promise save to bring you back in safety that worthless baggage, your daughter, and to say to my father that you do continue to be yourself, — and that is the tenderest mother and faithfullest wife, the loyallest subject, and most foolishly forgiving enemy in the province."

In Camp.

With this she swept a wide courtesy, and folding her mother in her arms kissed her on both cheeks.

"Here is one," quoth Fairfax to himself, "who knows no measure either in loving or hating. Perchance 'tis a pleasing nature to one at the right end of the gun, but to me, at the muzzle of her displeasure, 'tis a very vicious and altogether condemnable character."

The only vent of his reflections was in the tone of impatience which marked his next words: "Come, madam!"

"Go on, sir, and I will follow, as a captive should."

"Pardon me, but your place, both as a captive and a lady, is in front."

Not another word uttered My Lady Disdain as she swept down the dark hall. Fairfax, following, felt himself a belated Douglas with another captive queen on his hands. This princess knew so little of the humility demanded of a prisoner that she entered the dining-room with as high a mien as though she were lady of the manor, and these her retainers awaiting her pleasure. Her eye swept rapidly over the circle of men gathered about the table, whose polished top reflected their faces in grotesque foreshortening. They were marked faces all, and more marked than ever now, as the dim light of early dawn fell grayly on their features.

In the centre of the group, in a high arm-chair carved with heavy lion's heads, sat General Bacon, of figure indifferent tall, and somewhat over-slender for a man in perfect health. His deep-set eyes and overhanging brows lent to his countenance an aspect ominous, pensive, and melancholy, such as marks the portrait of every great man that has come down to us, strive as the painter may to hide it beneath a smiling lip or triumphant eye. The peaked beard and damp, dark hair straggling down across the high, white forehead contributed to form a strange likeness to the unfortunate Charles, — a likeness which haunted all who met this man, and perchance lent something to the magnetic power of his personal influence. Here was a king by divine right indeed, one who could rule the minds of men, — able to sway states to mighty issues. None could look on him and doubt it, though the choleric temper which showed in every glance of that quick eye might make the on-looker question whether here lay also that calm judgment and far-reaching grasp which could mould events as well as stir them.

Next to Bacon and a little behind him, so placed that his face lay in shadow, sat the subtle Mr. Lawrence, the man whose counsels had turned the tide of opinion on a doubtful day in the old field by the shores of the York River. His elbow rested on the table, and the hand on which his chin was propped so covered the close-shaven mouth that none could read its expression. It was a favorite attitude with him, and well revealed the character of the man. His curious, inscrutable opaque blue eyes, which saw much and told little, were fixed upon the girl so closely that in spite of herself her confidence faltered somewhat, and she turned her own gaze aside. In so doing it fell upon the figure of a young man at the farther side of the room. Little enough had he, one would have said, to merit the gathering intensity with which she regarded him. His loose lips, retreating chin, and shambling limbs marked only feebleness of will and fickleness of purpose. His color was sallow, and of a yellow pallor beneath the tan which the summer suns had bestowed upon it; but now, as Penelope Payne continued that fixed, scornful gaze, his cheeks became dyed with a deep, painful red, as though her look were a flame which burned him through and through. After one swift glance he had cast down his furtive eyes; but at length they rose again beneath the compelling power of her gaze.

"*You — here?*"

These were all the words she said; but a volume could not have uttered more amazement and contempt. The youth writhed on his chair as though it had been a pillory, twisting one foot about the other ankle, then untwining it and shuffling both feet about the floor, striving all the time to find words, till at last in very pity Mr. Lawrence was moved to speak for him.

"Yes, Mistress Payne, your cousin has of late seen the business of this controversy so clearly that he has been driven by reason and conscience to join himself to the followers of General Bacon. I would that all others of his kin might show themselves so wise as to follow his good example."

"Perchance," added Bacon, "he may be able to convert one this day. 'T is thy cousin, mistress, who is commissioned to be thine escort to James City; for I do presume it will meet thy wish more nearly to have him than a stranger to bear thee company."

"Nay," answered the girl, "spare me such insult. Send whom you will, but tie not my bridle rein to that of a Judas!"

The youth cringed as though a lash had struck him. There are whips whose whistle is never heard in the air, and stripes borne for life that no outward eye can take note of.

"Hard words those, young lady," quoth one who had not spoken till now. "May not a man claim freedom to join one side or the other as he sees fit without having such names as 'Judas' cast upon him?"

"Ay, some men may," answered Penelope, never flinching; "some men, but not Arthur Thorn, — not he whom my father brought up under his own roof, whom my mother cherished and cared for, and who not six months since prayed me to accept the precious offering of his heart and hand. A fine figure he doth make now, forsooth, driven by his reason and conscience to fight against his benefactor, to imprison the woman above stairs to whom he owes everything, and to ride as a jailor beside her whom half a year ago he besought to be his wife."

An awkward silence followed these scathing words. At length Bacon broke it, saying: "For your private grievances, Mistress Payne, you must e'en find private settlement. Our minds are overfull of public matters of great moment to permit of our entering upon a trial in a court of love."

Penelope bowed haughtily and vouchsafed no other response. After a moment Bacon continued: "I sent yesterday, as you know, to secure the presence in camp of your mother; and though I did not send for you, and Fairfax unduly exceeded his commission in permitting you to accompany her, yet now am I well content, since you, better perhaps than any other, can do our errand in yonder town."

"And what may that errand be?"

"All in good time, young lady. Permit me to speak without breaking in and you shall the sooner be enlightened. I would have you bear word to Governor Berkeley that our earthworks are not yet finished, and that we, therefore, request him of his courtesy to make no attack before noon."

Penelope's short lip curled shorter than ever. "'T is little ye must know of the Governor's nature that ye send him such a message by the mouth of a maid. Think ye he will come cap in hand, bowing low and saying with civil flourishes: 'Gentlemen, kindly let me know when you do be quite in readiness, that I may move upon your works with all ceremony'?"

The mockery of the tone in which this was uttered brought a sullen flush to Lawrence's face.

"Teach the minx her place!" he whispered in the ear of his chief; but Bacon shook his head. "Let it not be said," he answered, "that a girl hath power to vex a soldier." Then turning once more to Penelope, he said gravely, yet with a twinkle in his solemn eyes which was like sunshine behind a black cloud: "From what I do know of Governor Berkeley, I should expect his answer to be so little like what you have set forth that it might be quite unmeet for the ear of a lady."

"Ay, I will answer for it that it would, and more than that, — it would be delivered by the cannons' mouth rather than his own."

"Of a truth I doubt it not. 'T is the very thing I have foreseen, and thereunto have we taken our precautions. I desire, therefore, that with your other message you do tell His Excellency that we have decided to place Madam Ballard, Madam Bacon, and Madam Bray, together with your mother, in front of our fortifications till they be completed; and say to him that we trust consideration for the safety of these ladies, if not for our wishes, will lead him to delay his untimely advance."

Penelope Payne grew white, and seized the casement of the door; but her spirit did not quail.

"Cowards!" she cried, facing them like a lioness at bay, "let your cause win or lose, it shall be said of you far and wide that ye were poltroons who dared not fight like men, but must needs shelter yourselves behind the white aprons of women."

Bacon in his turn whitened at the word '*coward*.' But Lawrence muttered: "Parley no more with the saucy baggage! We are wasting precious time. Bid her be off!"

Bacon had rallied ere Lawrence ceased speaking. "Major Fairfax," he said, "is all in readiness?"

"All is in readiness."

"You are fully armed?"

"I have my sword and pistols."

"'T is well. Whatever haps you must not be taken till your message be delivered. My orders are that you accompany this young lady to James City, where, having said her say, you may leave her in safety among her friends."

At this for the first time Penelope's courage broke down utterly, and the tears ran down her pale cheeks.

"Ah, General, you are strong; be also merciful! Say but that I may return to be with my mother, and forget my hasty words of a moment since!"

The girl would fain have knelt before him, but he raised her, his own features working strongly with emotion. "Thou art a brave maid and a good daughter," quoth he, "and thou shalt have thy will. If thou canst persuade thy father to hear to thy return, I will not forbid it. But now to horse, and that with speed!"

With deep respect General Bacon led Penelope

to the door and set her upon the horse which had stood tethered to a tree hard by. Fairfax made her stirrup right and tightened the girth of her saddle. So they set forth, thus for the second time within twenty-four hours strangely forced into companionship.

The chipmunk stopped in his wild gallop up and down the tree-trunk, and turned his head to watch them passing, till his little black, bead-like eyes could see no farther. The crested bittern flapped her wings in friendly fashion over their heads, and the chattering plover gossiped in their ears the secrets of his love, as though, forsooth, his instinct were gone so far astray as to tell him that these two were lovers with hearts in tune to all the loves of the world around them. Strange sarcasm of Fate! While these human beings rode on surrounded by joy, and love, and peace, their own souls were filled with thoughts of war, and hatred, and bitterness.

At length, heralded by the bursting forth of all nature into a pæan of song and bloom, up rose the red September sun, full and round and fiery, foretelling another day of heat and drouth.

"Methinks the earth is well-nigh parched for want of rain." Fairfax ventured this remark as one who holds out an olive branch. It was not accepted. Mistress Payne but held her head the higher, and pressed her lips the closer, and strained her eyes, as though striving to catch a glimpse of the gates of James City, where she might make an end of his hateful guardianship.

Fairfax was no long-suffering saint, — only an honest and well-meaning fellow, with a great reverence for all women, and a mighty tenderness for one in misfortune. Had his advance been more civilly met, he would have been glad of the chance to speak his sympathy; but now he forced it all back, and told himself that he cared not a farthing what befell this lofty young woman, who, for the matter o' that, would but be the better for a little humbling.

Thus they rode on in silence, at once so near together and so far asunder, till at length a turn in the road brought Jamestown full in view, though distant still across the long, flat reaches of Virginia marsh-land. There rose the tower of the old church. There peeped the roof of the powder magazine, and borne to them on the still morning air came the shrilling of the fife, answered by the deep rumbling of the gruff drum.

"Faith," thought Fairfax, "we are arrived none too soon. A little later and Berkeley's troops would have been on the move, and we might have missed them at the fork in the road behind us. What would the General have done had he seen the enemy actually moving on his works? What *would* he have done?"

"*Crack!*" sounded a gun. A flash of flame and a curl of smoke from the bushes told Fairfax that he had been taken off his guard by one of Berkeley's pickets. Instantly, as his quick eye noted that the firing came from the side of the road nearest Penelope Payne, he wheeled the horses so that she was sheltered, and taking aim at the smoke still curling through the underbrush he fired. At the same moment another shot came whizzing through the air, and Fairfax's bridle arm dropped useless at his side.

"For the love of God," cried Fairfax, "ride on! ride for your life! Should I fall, stay not to help me, but ride the swifter. There be more lives than thine or mine at stake!"

So saying, he struck his spurs deep into his horse's side, and the two started on a full gallop, though the blood had soaked through his sleeve and trickled down in a red line upon his stocking.

On and on sped the horses, now perforce slowing up a little to pick their way over the rough corduroy road of logs laid loosely over the bog, then dashing over the bridge, their hoofs echoing noisily against the planks. The gate was gained at last.

"Halt!" cried the sentry. "No farther, though ye bore twenty flags of truce, till ye do tell your errand!"

"We must see Governor Berkeley," said Fairfax; but his voice sounded faint in his own ears.

"Come ye as friends or foes?"

"Both. I am a follower of Bacon; but this young lady is the daughter of Colonel Payne."

"Who speaks my name without there?" asked a deep, authoritative voice over the sentry's shoulder.

"Father!" cried Penelope. Even as she spoke Fairfax fell forward on his horse's neck, faint with loss of blood.

CHAPTER III.

FLAG OF TRUCE.

"The Latin tongue seems somewhat injurious to the female sex: for whereas *amicus* is a friend, *amica* always signifies a sweetheart; as if their sex were not capable of any other kind of familiar friendship but in way to marriage."

"COWARDS!"

"Miscreants!"

"Dogs of rebels!"

"An I had my way they should be blown from the mouth of the cannon when we reach Green Spring."

Fairfax stood leaning against the wall of the powder magazine, listening with outward calmness to the bitter outcry raised by all the excited folk in James City when Penelope Payne had delivered her message. When first he had regained consciousness after his swoon, the surgeon was binding his arm, and no one else at hand; for all were gathered about the group where stood Governor Berkeley with Colonel Payne and his daughter. Penelope oft cast furtive glances at the surgeon as he worked, but her attention was quickly reclaimed by the eager exclamations around her.

Fairfax, full of inward curses over his own weakness, declined the doctor's offer to help him into Major Beverley's house which stood hard by; but he drank deep of a cup of spirits, and then, rising, drew near the group of talkers.

In its centre stood Sir William Berkeley.

He was a stalwart and a doughty knight, for all his threescore years and ten. His hair, which fell in a queue upon his shoulders, was bleached by nature and age, whiter than all the powder in the three kingdoms could have made it, and its thickness was greater than that of bag-wig, full-bottomed tie, or curly peruke.

The eye that flashed beneath the shaggy gray eyebrow had neither the dimness nor the coldness of age. It was fiery, choleric, vengeful; and now, dilated as it was with passion, it seemed a bale-fire able to consume the mob of miscreants who dared to dispute his autocratic will. The tumult of rage within him stirred even the breastplate of steel which he still wore, when most had abandoned armor as heavy and useless; but to this man all that savored of the past was sacred, and he asked but to live and die in the traditions of his ancestors.

Flag of Truce.

Fairfax stood a moment unobserved; but as the crowd swayed to and fro, Berkeley caught sight of him, and all his pent-up rage burst forth. His face turned from red to purple, and the veins of his forehead swelled till those about feared to see him fall in a fit.

"I'll teach you," he cried, shaking his fist in the face of Fairfax, "I'll teach you to come with such messages to me. Beverley, order out the guard and have the pestilent fellow shot."

At this Penelope Payne took a step forward and opened her lips as if about to speak; but her father was before her.

"Nay, nay! Your Excellency," he said, laying his hand soothingly on Sir William's cuff. "You mean not all you say; you would be the last man to order a flag of truce violated."

"And you say this?" asked Berkeley, between wrath and amazement. "You, whose wife these wretches propose to set up as a shield betwixt themselves and our bullets? Faith, if good old Dr. Fuller thought it strange that the devil's black guard should be enrolled God's soldiers, he might e'en think it stranger still could he see these innocent dames thus entered as a white guard to the devil."

"If General Bacon plays the part of coward he

must bear the scorn and contumely which his acts do call for; but let us not cast ourselves under the same reproach by the breaking of honorable rules of civilized warfare. Besides, this young man is not responsible for the doings of his superior officer, — our revenge should fall not on him, but on Bacon."

"Ay," shouted a rough-looking man on the outskirts of the crowd. "Let us be revenged on Bacon; I vote for an immediate attack."

Colonel Payne turned upon the speaker with fire in his glance. "Wretch!" cried he. "Think ye that to pierce our enemy's side we will dart our weapons through the breasts of our wives?"

A murmur of mingled applause and disapprobation ran about the crowd at these words. While Colonel Payne was speaking, the Governor was striding up and down, well-nigh beside himself with fury, ever and anon clutching at the hilt of his sword as though he had a mind to run Fairfax through with his own hand, then glaring at him contemptuously as though he found him unworthy such honor.

Fairfax neither spoke nor moved, but stood there still as a stone image. He looked a thorough soldier, though the light locks which in old Saxon days had given his family its name fell on his shoulders in curls, and though his eyes were blue as any maid's that caught their color from the cornflower; yet the softness which these bespoke was contradicted by the haughty bearing, the resolute mouth, and the fighting chin thrust combatively forward beyond the upper jaw. White and wan as he was, and with one hand disabled and carried in a sling, Bryan Fairfax was yet not a man to be trifled with. The steady gaze wherewith he now confronted Berkeley was as free from fear as the Governor's own, and as cool as Berkeley's was hot. Its very calmness more enraged the man before him than any anger could have done.

"Am I master here, or am I not?" cried the Governor, looking from one to another. "Is there none to do my bidding?"

At the moment a swaying of the crowd marked the efforts of some one to force a passage, and a stout halberdier elbowed his way to the front, and behind him, holding her head high and somewhat scornfully, walked Lady Frances Berkeley. Apparently unmoved by the tumult around her, she walked calmly to her husband's side and laid her hand upon his cuff. Not a word said she, only stood looking at him as one that knew this mood of old and had learned how best to meet it. Gradually his fingers relaxed their clutch at the hilt of his sword, then the hand fell away from the weapon and laid itself upon that other hand on his cuff. His eyes lost their fierceness, and took on instead a wholly human look of tenderness and affection, which so transformed his countenance that it seemed to bring back his old nature with all its old-time gentlehood.

"Why, how now, poppet?" said His Excellency, in a tone so soft that one who had heard him but now addressing Fairfax could scarce have believed it was the same man who spoke. Those who stood around (especially the women) smiled behind their hands at the word "poppet" addressed to the middle-aged, tight-lipped little lady, trim and prim, carrying her chin stiffly above the starched ruff with a touch-me-not air which might well have made this pet name seem somewhat comical to those who realized not that true love hangs wreaths of roses on its idol though it be of iron, and that an idol never grows old.

"What brings thee here?" added Berkeley. "Get thee home. 'T is no place for women, though there be too many here. Let them but fancy they are not wanted and they will face the culverin."

"Ay, that will I," answered My Lady, "when thou art there to protect me."

Thus did she, who dearly loved a fight, whom indeed Dame Rumor credited with having provoked more than one with the weapon of her tongue, and who would not have flinched before the whole rebel army, play upon her husband's weakness, knowing full well, perchance, that love has its interruptions, but that vanity is perpetual.

Berkeley swelled up at her words to a still more inflated dignity; but the growing softness in his eye showed his lady that her cause was won.

"I was fain," she added, "to look nearer upon this Fairfax to whom I heard ye speaking a few minutes since, for I was mightily curious to know if it was that Bryan Fairfax who is reported the best sportsman in Warwick County."

Here again the shrewdness of the dame peeped forth, for she knew full well that the Governor loved a sportsman as he hated a rebel. Berkeley himself felt his resentment weaken, and made a desperate effort to recover it. "I know not what or how much ye may have heard of this Bryan Fairfax, my lady, — all I know or wish to know is that he is my prisoner."

"Nay," answered Lady Berkeley, smiling up into Sir William's bloodshot eyes, but extending her hand to Fairfax, who was in truth an old favorite of hers before these war times and well remembered at the hunt balls, — "nay, I swear he is *my* prisoner!"

"Say rather, your slave," answered Fairfax, who had a mighty pretty wit of his own and kept it close behind his tongue.

"Take him, then," cried Sir Turkey Cock, swelling stouter and redder than ever. "Take him, and wrap him in wool if ye like, to be ready for the next fox hunt; but for us whose business is to hunt men, 't is time to be about our preparations."

"Then must I beg another escort of Your Excellency that I may return with all speed to Green Spring."

So spoke the voice of Penelope Payne, who had been standing by, less noticed than her youthful vanity fully relished in a scene wherein she had thought to play the heroine.

"Zounds!" cried Sir William. "What have we here! Payne, has your daughter turned rebel too in these days when all the world is upside down, or is she gone mad that she doth imagine we will consent to send her back to be but one more target for our bullets? That red head of thine," he added, turning toward Penelope and speaking more kindly, "were too fair a mark."

"My daughter is right," said Colonel Payne, speaking with slow utterance and with that dryness of the throat which marks intense inward feeling. "Come good, come ill, her place is beside her mother. Mistress Berkeley, I petition thee that this prisoner of thine who hath brought my daughter safely hither may be her guardian on the return journey."

"'T were willingly done on my part," answered Lady Berkeley, "if so be my husband giveth his leave."

"'Sdeath," cried the Governor, "if you are all bound to use the golden rule as a ramrod, the sooner we open our gates to the rebels the better. On your own heads be the result of your folly! I wash my hands of the business!"

With this His Excellency turned in high dudgeon, and folding his arms behind his back, like one resolved both in letter and spirit to have no hand in the matter, he strode on; or, to speak more graphically, strutted off. Colonel Payne stood looking dubiously after him, knowing not how to interpret his behavior; but Lady Berkeley whispered: "'T is a compromise. He will not say 'Yea,' but he hath not said, 'Nay.' Off with them ere his mood harden!"

The Colonel bowed assent. He drew his daughter to his breast and held her there close, close as though he never could let her go. The slow tears fell from the man's stern eyes upon the girl's bright hair. At last with one final embrace he released her; then taking her hand he placed it in that of Fairfax, saying solemnly, —

"The Lord do so to you, and more also, as you do unto this my child!"

They were strange words to pass between enemies. On the instant it shot through the minds of those who stood around that this was like to the ancient form of betrothal. But the words which next fell from the father's lips were in quite another spirit.

"I would, Major Fairfax, that I might break my mind to your General, but you in my stead may say to him from me, as Governor Berkeley's commanding officer, that, being gentlemen, we would no sooner fire at women than we would shelter ourselves behind them. We will wait for his fortifications to be finished, presuming that he intends not to fight his whole campaign behind 'White Aprons.'"

A titter ran about the group at the last words, and the angry color mantled Fairfax's cheek.

"Silence!" commanded Colonel Payne, looking sharply from man to man.

"Say also," he continued, "to General Bacon, that I consider the insult he hath thus put upon my wife and daughter to be doubly an insult to me, and that meet him where I may, in war or peace, on the battle-field, or in the council hall, I will shoot him like the beast he is."

"O Father, Father!" sobbed the girl, clinging closer to him.

"Nay, nay, my darling! Have no fears. Methinks 'tis but a cowardly ruse on Bacon's part and that he doth intend no bodily harm, but in any case bethink thee that thou art a soldier's daughter, and bear thyself as one who fears naught that men can do."

They were almost the very words her mother had uttered as they turned their backs on the dear walls of Rosemary, and the flood of recollection sadly shook the firmness still left to Penelope.

A tumult of wrath and resentment shook the soul of the man who stood by her side. In all his honorable young life Fairfax had never till this day known what it meant to be scorned, and now he could ill brook the looks of contempt and ill will which met his gaze on every side.

"Colonel Payne," he answered, striving to keep his voice steady, "I can answer for the safe conduct of your daughter and the safe bearing of your message. The slur upon General Bacon you are secure in casting, here in your stronghold, where

I am as powerless to retort as to avenge. When we meet again, I trust my sword may speak for me."

Colonel Payne bowed a haughty acknowledgment of these words the while he busied himself with setting his daughter on her horse. When she had made ready, Fairfax climbed into his own saddle; and though the wounded arm hindered him not a little, none offered him help. Amid a silence which spoke louder than groans or curses, he adjusted the bridle reins of the two horses, then he and his charge rode slowly through the lines of hostile faces, rode through the gate grudgingly opened by hostile hands, rode across the echoing bridge, then out into the open country, stretching away free and clear to Green Spring.

Ah, what a relief to turn from all the turmoil of human passions to the tranquillity of Nature, whose face smiles not a whit the less, though contending armies shed blood upon her garments!

Bryan Fairfax within the last two hours had faced the wrath of armed men, the suffering of a wound, the chance of death itself; yet none of these were so keenly in his mind as the rebuff with which the girl beside him had met his attempted kindness. It is the little things of life which make it bitter or sweet.

Thus Major Fairfax rode on in resolute silence,

looking straight before him, as one bent only on fulfilling his distasteful commission, and in haste to be relieved of his troublesome duty of guard.

"Poor Papa! It wrung his heart to let me go."

Fairfax started as though a cannon had been discharged at his ear. He could scarce credit his own hearing when it told him that his companion had of her own volition broken the hostile silence which had lain betwixt them. For an instant he paused, watchful of his dignity, as youth ever is, and hesitated whether or no to accept the olive branch thus held out to him.

"In sooth," he answered at last, "it could have been no otherwise, yet was his counsel according to the wisdom for which he is reputed, and he bore himself to the end like the brave man he is."

"Yet you would shoot him if you met this day," said the girl, somewhat tremulously; for I must confess here, almost at the beginning of my tale, that Penelope Payne was no iron heroine, no Joan of Arc, but a very human and altogether variable maiden, who could be touched to compassion or keyed to heroism, but who cared little for principles or causes as compared with people. Having once vented her hot temper, she found it increasingly difficult to preserve the chill disapprobation which lingers so easily with colder natures. Besides, the thought perpetually and importunately knocked at her heart, "He risked his life to save mine."

Fairfax was quick to feel the hint of softening, as she rushed on after her wonted impetuous fashion: "Why do you, why should any one, hate my father?" Of a sudden the fiery brown eyes were drowned in tears as a realization of the meaning of war swept over her for the first time, bringing in its train the thought of blood and wounds, of suffering and death.

"Be of good heart, Mistress Payne," answered Fairfax, a hint of irony in his tone; "ye need have little fear for your father from any enmity of mine. He is a veteran, and far liker to shed my blood than I his."

The girl shuddered. "Oh!" cried she, "belike it is because I am a woman and have a woman's weakness that war do seem so horrible in mine eyes. For the life of me I cannot comprehend why and wherefore all the sons of the Dominion are fallen of a sudden to cutting each the others' throats."

"Wherefore indeed!" sighed Fairfax, more as 't were thinking aloud than answering his companion. "Were it not for the diabolical temper of one man, the colony would be in peace and unity, with no foes but those without."

Penelope Payne stretched that long throat of hers still longer, and held her head high and stiffly, with a swift change from the half-friendliness of a moment before. A spiritual thermometer would have marked a fall of forty degrees in the warmth of her manner as she said, "You speak, I presume of General Bacon."

Fairfax felt a swift pang of regret that he had been drawn on to break the truce between them; but the girl's tone stirred his anger, and with the eager unwisdom of youth he took up the glove of controversy.

"Nay," said he, "not of Bacon, but of one who hath wronged him at every turn. General Bacon did ask naught save the poor boon of permission to defend his home and the homes of all of us against the savages who are lurking in the wood like so many wild beasts, ready to leap out upon us as they did on our grandfathers fifty years ago, when the settlers thought themselves so secure. But Bacon is too good a soldier to await the pleasure of the enemy and let them take their own time for opening the fight. Oh, his foes will yet be forced to own him the greatest man of our time, — scholar, soldier, statesman, and gentleman!"

The girl's tone was hot with anger as she made answer: "A soldier certainly, a scholar perchance, but a *gentleman*—never! How dare you call one 'gentleman' who sets up women as targets above his works. Oh, of a truth, Bacon and the rest of you shall be set forever in the pillory of public contempt as 'White Aprons'!"

The laugh which followed these words was bitter, and grated on the ear of him who heard it. An older man would have met the thrust and parried it with that contemptuous toleration which most chafes the hot and angry heart; but Fairfax was young, and the semblance of truth in the girl's words stung him to the quick. "There," cried he, snatching a paper from the breast of his coat and thrusting it out toward Penelope Payne; "read that, and confess with shame how unjust you have been!"

Penelope took the paper and read. It was an official order hastily written on a half-sheet of paper.

"MAJOR FAIRFAX,"—it ran,—"You will take charge of the women lately captured and brought to the camp. They are to be stationed upon the little hill in front of our works, in order that in the event of Berkeley's approach they may be seen from afar. Should Berkeley, however, so far forget every natural scruple as to order an advance on the works, it will be your duty to see that the women are withdrawn at once to a place of safety, and that under no circumstances are they allowed to sustain any, the least, injury.

"(Signed) NATHANIEL BACON."

The relief to Penelope's overstrained nerves was almost too great. Her fear for her mother set so suddenly at rest, her anxieties for the moment lulled, she bowed her head upon the high pommel of her saddle, and wept bright tears wherein the world around seemed to dance in rose-colored reflections.

When she at length raised her head and opened her eyes, she turned toward Major Fairfax with a look of friendliness such as her face had not yet worn for him. She held out the paper to him with a dazzling smile; but it met impenetrable gloom. The young soldier's brow was knit, his cheeks flushed, and he gnawed nervously at his under lip.

"Are you angry with me?" asked the girl, a note of timidity for the first time in her voice.

"No, with myself," he answered. "I have done that which merits the loss of my rank, perhaps worse. I have betrayed orders which if not marked secret, were assuredly never meant to meet your eye. In short, I have been a fool."

"Nay, Major Fairfax, unless to let in a ray of sunshine on the dark path of a poor maiden well-nigh distraught with trouble be foolishness, you have committed no folly. I swear to you that I will guard this secret as jealously as you yourself could do, holding it my very own. Why need any ever know that other eyes than yours have looked upon the order?"

"Because I am not a poltroon nor a deceiver," answered Fairfax, hotly, venting some of his impatience with himself upon his comrade, in very unheroic but highly human fashion. "You rate me as baser than I am, baser than you have called me yet, — though your tongue has not spared my poor character, — if you fancy I would withhold the knowledge of the breach of confidence whereof I have been guilty from General Bacon. For your mother and the rest, you must do as you think fit, — I will not stoop to ask you to keep a secret which I was too weak to guard myself."

With this Fairfax set the horses in a gallop, and they cleared the ground at so round a pace that the woods seemed to fly past them. Both man and maid were so wrapped in their own thoughts that it was with surprise that they found themselves passing the sentry, riding up the long avenue, and standing before the mansion of Green Spring. Not a soul was waiting to receive them. The grove was filled with soldiers, but not a person was about the house save the black servant waiting to take the horses. Fairfax turned to help Mistress Payne to alight; but as on the night before, she had slipped from her saddle without his aid. Quite simple and unconscious she stood there, tired and dusty and worn, less fair than she had looked a score of times ere now; but for some inscrutable reason the picture of her as she stood thus against the pillar entered into the heart of Bryan Fairfax never to be obliterated. As he looked at her, a new power came into his life. *He fell in love*, though as yet he guessed it not himself.

'T is a strange business, this falling in love; mysterious as the creation of the world. God says to the human soul, "Let there be light!" and there is light. That is all we know of it; and none of all those who have experienced the mystery can explain it to another.

Penelope Payne trembled a little, as one who feels the air electric with some strange new disturbing element but half comprehended. Stretching forth her hand and looking into his face, with eyes half appealing and wholly maidenly, she said:

"If you and I were not sworn enemies, I would say, 'Be my friend.'"

"May I?" he asked, bending low over her hand as though he were craving a boon so far above his deserts that he wondered at his own temerity.

You think perhaps that this was an over-sudden leap into love from the enmity and indifference of a few hours ago. "How did it come to pass?" you ask.

It came to pass because youth and love are stronger than all the wars and hatreds and estrangement between kindred,—and so runs the world away.

CHAPTER IV.

HEARTS OF GOLD.

"Form in rank; form in rank;
 Then move forward and outflank.
 Let me see them overpowered,
 Hacked, demolished, and devoured!
 Neither earth nor sea nor sky
 Nor woody fastnesses on high
 Shall protect them if they fly."

THE sun streamed full into the open window of the dining-room at Green Spring. It played cheerily on the dresser, around the silver marked with the Berkeley arms and over the row of pewter plates set on edge along the shelf. It glanced across the floor and climbed the twisted legs of the heavy chairs. It even entered daringly the open mouths of the lions' heads which formed the end of the arms and changed their fierce gaping to a harmless yawn.

One thing only they could not touch to cheerfulness, — the face of the man who stood with head bent and elbow propped against the mantel. Now that he was alone, its gravity and sadness were more marked than ever. The brows were knit, and the lines which curved downward from the nostril — lines which speak controlled nervousness — were still more deeply graven.

He sighed, not the sigh of sorrow, but the pant of a soul overloaded by the weight of mighty issues which it finds itself physically unequal to sustain. Such a sigh is the protest of mind against the hampering limitations of body.

As though the pent-up weariness were relieved by the expression thereof, Bacon's face lightened somewhat of its cloud, and still more as his ear caught the lively sound of fife and drum commanding the troops to gather.

"Ha!" said he, half aloud. "The men have finished the works sooner than I believed possible. Now let Berkeley come on when he will; we are ready for him. 'T is the hour of ten, if that tall Dutch clock in the corner speaks truth. Where the devil is Fairfax?"

As if answering to his name at roll-call, Bryan Fairfax appeared at the open door. Bacon's eye fell on the bandaged arm. His gloomy eye flashed fire.

"Have ye met foul play? By Heaven, they shall pay for it that dared such wrong!"

The youth before him was too much occupied

with the load on his conscience to heed the words. Scarce pausing for the military salute, he burst out with his confession.

Bacon looked grave the while he listened. "I had thought you trustworthy, Fairfax," he said at last; and his tone of withdrawal cut the younger man to the heart. "Up till now I have ever found ye as close-mouthed as one of the oysters in Chesapeake Bay; an I heard it not from your own lips I would ne'er have credited the story that ye had been pricked into the betrayal of a confidence by the pin point of a shrewish tongue."

The hot blood rushed over Fairfax's face and mounted to the roots of his hair. General Bacon noted it, and his tone softened somewhat as he continued: "Well, well, Major, ye have shown yourself a gallant officer in the field, which must in some measure expiate your fault, and your frank confession must be counted still further extenuation. Happily, this time your indiscretion hath wrought little harm, for the work here is done. The defences are finished, and we are ready for the worst Berkeley can design against us. Damn my blood!" he shouted, a sudden tide of passion sweeping over him; "I'll kill Governor, Council, Assembly and all, and then I'll sheathe my sword in my own heart's blood!"

When Bacon was in a mood like this, he was as one possessed. Fairfax stood stock-still, watching till the fit should pass. At last he ventured: "And what of the women?"

"Damn me!" cried Bacon, his anger rising once more at the mention of the sore subject. "I've done with these women, and the sooner they be gone the better; for if they tarry here much longer, *all* my officers may be corrupted from their loyalty."

"General Bacon, I am a gentleman, and I will be spoke to like one!" Though it was but a junior and a subordinate who uttered the words, Bacon felt the dignity of the tone and the justness of the reproach.

"Nay, nay," he said, laying his hand on the Major's shoulder, "take not so seriously what I spake in hot blood. I have told you already that I count your fault extenuated by its confession. Moreover, your wounded arm bears witness to your brave and faithful discharge of your trust; and as for being led away by a woman, ye have been no weaker than our forbear Adam in the Garden of Eden. Nor need ye look so far for justification, for by Heaven, our royal master on t' other side the sea sets us all a fine example."

"Hm!"

Both Bacon and Fairfax started at the sound of the suppressed cough, and looking up they saw a man's figure at the door which opened toward the kitchen passage.

"'T is that snake, Thorn!" muttered Fairfax.

"Ay, but I'll draw the poison of his fangs," said Bacon. Then turning toward Thorn: "Pray have ye any fault to find with my words?"

"Nay; surely a general may say what he will, though 't were flat treason from his subordinates."

"I prithee, good Master Thorn, since you count it mannerly to listen to a conversation never intended for your ears, will you be good enough to explain the kernel of treason which as you do imply lay hidden in my discourse? My words were that the King set us all a fine example. Say you not so?"

"Ay, of a truth!"

"Then have ye said all I said, and ye may go squeal it in Berkeley's ears; for as I live, I will send you over to the enemy's camp trussed like a stuck pig, when the battle is done, if ever you venture unbidden into my presence again, and thrust your impudent nose into matters that concern you not. Be gone, sir!"

Arthur Thorn meeched from the room; but as he

passed Fairfax, he cast on him a look of deadly hatred. "I did see it all," he muttered.

"Saw what? You infernal, prating liar!" cried Fairfax. "Speak, or I'll shake the falsehood out of you!"

"Saw what?" echoed Thorn mockingly. "I saw her extend her hand. I saw you take it and bend over it. Oh, I doubt not you had a charming morning's ride!"

The man's face was livid with baffled jealousy, mixed with malice and cowardice.

Ere the words were out of his mouth, Fairfax took him by the collar, and, raising him from the ground, shook him as I have seen a mastiff shake a mongrel. So beside himself with rage was Fairfax that he was like to have done his adversary some serious bodily harm; but Bacon's arm of authority was thrust between them, and his masterful voice said sternly: "Quarrelling like schoolboys! and in my presence! This passes. I will have you both in the guard-house and this cease not on the instant. Ye think, perchance, because the Governor hath withheld my commission, I am but the leader of a mob, a mad fellow with a motley crew of followers entitled to neither respect nor show of authority. By Heaven!—"

When he was advanced so far in his speech, the

red which had mantled his face changed to deep crimson, almost to purple, and he staggered and would have fallen but that his hand chanced to meet the lion's head, and grasping it for support he sank into the chair.

The behavior of the two young men matched with their character. Arthur Thorn, seizing his opportunity, sidled out through the open door, muttering to himself: "The storm may blow over, but some of us are like to be struck by lightning first."

Bryan Fairfax rushed forward and threw himself on his knees before Bacon in a very passion of remorse and contrition.

"Strike me!" he cried. "Stab me with the poniard in your belt! But for the love of God, look not like this upon me! I cannot bear it."

The anger died slowly out of Bacon's face, and a smile, or rather a sad and bitter shadow of a smile, followed it.

"What better should I look for?" he asked, speaking half to himself. "Do not rats desert a sinking ship, — and what but a rotten and timber-crazed craft am I?"

"Thou! Verily thou art the main prop and stay of the best cause and the goodliest country of the round world!"

Bacon shook his head.

"Tell me, does aught ail thee? I saw thee but now clutch at thy heart like one in mortal weakness"

"Nay, nay. 'T was but a passing giddiness. But it needs not that to strengthen my assurance. Fairfax, I am a doomed man."

"My God, General! What can have set thee on to such gloomy thoughts? Surely no man ever faced the cannon's mouth with such a cool front as thou."

"A cannon! Pooh! 'T were a coward indeed who feared to face a friendly ball of iron which but bids one good day in passing, and either leaves him unharmed or wafts him away in a twinkling to some less troublous world. But to feel one's self day by day less full of life and vigor, to will and find no answering action, to rub the brow till the flesh smarts, yet rouse not the drowsy thought, to stretch aching limbs in the morning and prod a reluctant frame to rise and meet the daily task, — to do all this, I say, and yet 'bate nothing of heart and hope, would tax more heroic stuff than I can boast."

"But how can this be true of you? — of you of all people in the world? — who go about heartening the men to their tasks, so full of courage that the ranks stand straighter when ye have passed? 'T is some strange freak of your fancy bred by the lack of sleep. You *must* have rest."

"'T is too late to cry 'Hold hard!' when the arrow has left the bow, and, Fairfax — you are the only man to whom I have breathed it, and I charge you hint it to no man living — but I count my symptoms too strange for natural illness. *I fear poison.*"

"Poison! My God!" cried Fairfax, turning white.

"Ay, slow poison, brewed from some of these deadly plants which do abound together with the healing herbs in the Virginia forests. Berkeley is desperate, and our game was nearly won. But if I die, 't is lost again, though all the dice of Fate show doubles. Drummond will ne'er serve under Lawrence — still less Lawrence yield precedence to Drummond. I would to God, Fairfax, thou hadst a few more years on that head of thine, for thou wouldst be the properest leader of them all."

"Nay, my Chief, my dear, dear Chief! Speak not of any inheriting thy power. 'T were as vain for the eagle to bequeath his nest to the sparrow."

"*Rub a dub! Rub a dub! Rub a dub dub!*"

The rumble of the drum with its recall to the world of action broke in thus upon the talk of the two men, — sudden and sharp as the knocking at the gate upon the guilt of Macbeth. As Bacon heard it, he sprang to his feet like one to whom new life has been given, and began buckling on his sword. "Hark!" he cried. "'T is the signal for forming. I bade Drummond give the summons when he saw a cloud of dust in the direction of James City. Who spoke of death? *Life, life!* glorious life is in the song of the rattling drum and the shrilling of the fife."

So utterly was the whole look and bearing of the man changed by this new-born martial vigor that Fairfax rubbed his eyes and could scarce believe he was not the victim of some strange bewildering dream; but Bacon gave him little time to speculate on the transformation. "Follow me!" he cried, flinging wide the great door and stepping forth into the full sunlight of the porch.

The greensward was filled with the ranks of his men, and as they caught sight of their leader a mighty cheer broke forth, — a cheer which brought the women in the upper chamber to the window, full of anxious fear lest the cheer from their foe meant a groan from their friends. As Penelope Payne looked down, her eyes fell upon Fairfax, who stood at the foot of the steps looking up at his chief with a face so full of loyalty, of love and devotion and yet of sadness withal, that it made Penelope think of an old print of Saint Sebastian which hung over the chimney breast at Rosemary Hall.

An instant later Bacon himself moved forward and stood on the edge of the porch, and as she gazed on him she felt, in spite of herself, the force of that magnetic influence which this man had the power to exert on all who came within reach of the magic of his look and voice. Raising his hand with a gesture which struck a sudden silence through the throng, he began an address to his soldiers, speaking with rapid and impassioned utterance, as though his feeling were some mighty torrent striving to force its rushing way through a channel too limited to contain its volume.

"Gentlemen and fellow soldiers," he said, then paused and passed his eyes over the ranks with so keen and individualizing a glance that each man felt himself singled out and noted, "how am I transported with gladness to find you thus unanimous, bold and daring, brave and gallant! You have the victory before the fight, the conquest before the battle. I know you can and dare fight, while Berkeley and his men will scarce attempt to hold the field before you. When we have beaten them here we will pursue them to their place of refuge at Jamestown. Your hardiness will invite all the country as we march to come in and second you. The Indians we bear along with us shall be as so many motives to cause relief from every hand to be brought to you. As for your foes—" here such a tone of scorn filled his voice as called the indignant red to Penelope's cheek and wholly swept away the dawning sentiment of admiration. Luckily, perhaps, Bacon did not look up, and continued unconscious of the wrath above his head: "As for your foes, I say, the ignominy of their actions cannot but so much reflect upon their spirit as they will have no courage left to fight you. I know you have the prayers and well wishes of all the people in Virginia, while the others are loaded with their curses. Come on, my hearts of gold! He that dies in the field, lies in the bed of honor."

The shout which greeted these last words told how they had struck home.

"Hurrah! Hurrah! Hurrah!"

"Bacon forever!"

"Freedom or death!"

"To your guns, men!" cried Bacon, well pleased to see them thus wrought upon. "The enemy are approaching. To your guns, and give them a loyal welcome from the cannon's throat. To your guns!"

The answer to Bacon's words was the deep booming of the iron cannon which swept the

Jamestown road, and this in turn met a sharp response from the advance of Berkeley's army.

To the women in that upper chamber at Green Spring the hours that followed seemed years. The trees in front of their window hid the scene of the battle from their view; but ever and anon they caught the flash, and their ears were perpetually assailed by the booming of the cannon, the rattle of musketry, and the shouts, now here now there, as the fortunes of the battle changed.

Then at last a mighty yell broke upon them, a shout of "Bacon! Bacon!" and a rushing out from the gates as of a long-pent torrent told them but too plainly that their friends had wavered and broken, — and who could say what corpses lay along that bloody road down which pursuers and pursued were flying like the wind when on some bleak November day it whirls dust and leaves before it till the eyes are blinded and the breath is lost?

One heart alone in all those within the mansion could find room for a thought or a hope in favor of a rebel; but Penelope Payne, as she stretched forth from the window and caught a glimpse of the flying and the falling figures, cried softly, —

"Oh may God spare my father and put our foes to rout! Yet I would not that *all* should suffer."

Her heart might have softened still further

could she have followed the battle as it raged along the highway and straggled through the green fields now red with blood and trodden by hostile feet. She would have seen a motley rabble, which Berkeley had striven in vain to transform into an army, and now a wild mob with neither discipline nor any ruling thought save how to secure once more the shelter of those walls of James City from which they had come forth but a few hours since with braggart confidence, thinking to put Bacon's men to flight by the mere sight of their overwhelming force. But they had little known the character of those who fought against them and who came on with a mingled dash and discipline before which Berkeley's troops fled like chaff before the gale. In vain their gallant officers called to them to stand fast. In vain the few veterans closed together and led a desperate counter-charge. The main body was routed, the soldiers falling over each other in the madness of their stampede.

"Turn about!" cried Drummond, dashing like a whirlwind upon the flying foe — "turn about, and let us have a look at your white faces!"

"Look in my face, then, and see if it be white with fear of the like of you." Deep and steady came these words. The man who spoke them had stood like a rock, breasting the tide of retreat and striving to turn the mob rushing back to Jamestown.

He raised his pistol as he spoke and took cool aim at Drummond; but before he could fire Drummond swerved his horse, and at the same instant a troop of Bacon's men came flying around the turn of the road. A pistol shot was fired and struck Colonel Payne in the leg.

Surely he had fallen on that stubbly field never to rise again but that on the instant a gleam of recognition passed between him and the young officer who rode in front, his fair hair flying, his left arm bound to his breast.

"Halt!" cried Fairfax. "Touch him not, as you value your lives. 'Tis but this morning this man hath saved my life, and think ye I will see his taken thus? Colonel Payne," he added, turning to the grizzled warrior before him, from whose leg the blood was trickling in a dark stream, "'tis vain for one brave man to strive thus to stem the tide of battle. You have done all that valor could; to do more is foolhardiness. Get you on to this horse of my orderly and rejoin your men with what speed you may. Nay, never pause nor look so doubtfully! Hereafter you may meet me if you will in open combat on a fairer field, but it were scarce worthy of a Virginia gentleman did ye refuse to let me thus pay a debt of honor. What, hesitating still? — then I do adjure thee in the name of thy wife and daughter, who even now are praying on bended knees in yonder upper chamber for thy safety. Ah 't is well," he added, as he saw the Colonel soften at this appeal, "for there is no time to lose. Speed! Speed!" Then turning he cried aloud, "Come on, men! Let him go his way, and do you follow me up this road whither I saw Ludwell and his command in full retreat."

As they dashed forward, Fairfax whispered to himself: "To the end — war or no war!"

And at the same moment the lips of Penelope Payne, who stood gazing with strained vision from the window at Green Spring, were framing these very words.

There are certain crises in our lives when the soul is like the sensitive plate exposed for but an instant to the light, yet bearing ever after in its darkness the imprint of the vision caught within that moment. So it was with this maiden. She had looked for the first time into the eyes of love, had felt its glow, and caught the reflection at least of its glory. In an instant she had flung the darkness of her angry young heart betwixt her and the vision; but it was too late.

Not yet, however, would she have admitted any such thought; not while her mother lay a prisoner in that chamber behind her; not while her father perhaps stood in mortal peril from the weapon in the hand of the man whose image rose so importunately before her.

But when all this storm and stress had spent its force; when once more she sat alone before her spinet in the peace of Rosemary Hall; above all, when her father, who had brought home his wound to be nursed, told how he owed his life to Bryan Fairfax, — then the tide of feeling would no longer be restrained, but burst over every obstacle, and overflowed the girl's heart in a tempestuous wave of mingled hope and fear, joy and woe, pride and shame; while above all, like Arthur's sword, with keen edge and jewelled hilt, rose the longing to see *him* once more. So bright, and yet so sharp with anguish seemed the thought of meeting, that she could scarce tell if she wished or feared it most, but turned away her thoughts as from something she dared not look upon too near.

CHAPTER V.

A TRADER.

"Wilt thou give to me thy begging coat?
With a hey lillelu and a how lo lan.

"And I 'll give to thee my scarlet cloak,
And the birk and the broom blooms bonnie.

"Give me your auld pike-staff and hat,
With a hey lillelu and a how low lan.

"And ye sall be right weel paid for that,
And the birk and the broom blooms bonnie."

OF all the laughable absurdities and inconsistencies which beset our poor human nature, surely the passion of love is the strangest and most unaccountable in its freaks. No principles can control it, no prophet predict it, — prankish as Puck, wilful as a spoiled child, uncertain as the will o' the wisp on a summer's night. If there be any law governing it, it is the law of pure contrariness. It needs only that all influences be unfavorable to set it aflame, as the rubbing of stones strikes the spark for the savage. Let but the Montagues and Capulets be at daggers drawn, and straightway we have a Romeo and Juliet ready to see a curse fall on both their houses, if they may but live and love. So it has ever been; and so it now fell out as naturally, spontaneously, and inevitably in Virginia as in Verona.

Bryan Fairfax was conquered, not by Berkeley's guns, but by the white hand of Penelope Payne stretched out to him there at Green Spring and Penelope's voice bidding him be her friend. Weeks had passed since that day, — weeks of triumph for Bacon and his cause. Joy reigned in the hearts of all his followers — of *all?* No; for one it was not so. The gladness which would have bubbled over in shouts and jests aforetime with Fairfax was now sadly sobered by the thought that every gain to him was loss to one already dearer than himself. When he rode up the streets of Jamestown by the side of Bacon with banners flying, and saw the torch applied to the wooden houses and the old church, he could scarce bring himself to join in the cheers which burst forth from the invaders as the flames mounted to the sky in a devil's bonfire.

His comrades noted the change in him, and wondered much thereat. "What hath come over Fairfax?" asked one. "He that was the foremost fighter among us, gay as a lark, singing and shouting before the battle, is of a sudden turned womanish and pales at the sight of blood. But yesterday, when I would have kicked out of my way the body of a Berkeleyite lying stiff and stark by the roadside, Fairfax grasped my arm as though I were a murderer. 'Hate the living, if you must,' he cried, 'but spare your insults to the dead!'"

"Thou dost not think him a turncoat?"

"Nay, nay; none durst say such a word of Bryan Fairfax. Truer or braver heart never beat. I heard him say but yesterday, that he would shed the last drop of blood in his veins ere he would see our cause fail; yet the more victories we gain, the more he mopes."

"Oh, well, belike he hath a turn of trouble with the stomach, which doth oft cast down the heart; but when he hath had a dose of physic he will be glad as any. He cannot help it. Why, I tell thee, the child that is unborn shall have cause to rejoice for the good that will come by the rising of the country."

The quick ear of Fairfax caught a word or two of this and like discourse, and his proud and sensitive spirit chafed under it. He longed for some chance to prove his hearty loyalty, and he was glad when the opportunity came.

One night he was bidden to Bacon's tent. "Fairfax," said the General, as he entered, "I have difficult service on hand, difficult and dangerous. Knowst thou any man fit for the task and ready for its risks?"

"I know not if my powers be counted equal to its demands, but of a surety I am as little like as any man to be afear'd of its hazards if you will but honor me so far as to make trial of me therein."

"Ah!" answered Bacon. "'T was precisely thus I did hope thou wouldst be moved to answer, — though thy wound is so lately healed that thou mightst well crave excuse from dangerous service; but truth to tell, Fairfax, there is none I trust like thee. Nay, not even Lawrence, for all his subtlety and college breeding that he hath brought from over seas. Listen, then!" — and Bacon lowered his voice. "It hath come to my ears how Berkeley hath no less a treasure in his keeping than an order from the King for the delivery of my commission."

Fairfax started. "Ay," continued Bacon, "he hath been wont to keep it with him at Green Spring; but at the prospect of our coming last month, he did order it, with other papers of value, transported to the plantation of Colonel Robert Boynton, in the heart of the peninsula. 'T is a perilous attempt to secure it, yet 't would help mightily; for the chief cry against us is that we are disloyal to the King."

"Give me but a handful of men and we will make a raid on the place."

"Dost think we can afford to open so secret a business even to a few? No, — whosoever goes must go alone."

Fairfax paused as one who weighs his words and counts their cost; then he said quietly: "*I* will go, and if I come not again 't will be small loss save of the commission, and it shall go hard, but I contrive to rescue that."

"Nay, lad, it would grieve me more to lose you than the commission. I doubt not ye would make a bold fight; but 't is to your craft and coolness rather than your sword or gun that ye must trust. I have learned — ask me not how or whence — that the commission is concealed within the mansion itself, but in what portion thereof I know not. In the house dwell three bachelor kinsmen of Colonel Boynton. The three are widely famed for their giant strength and their skill in fighting. Two of them have joined Berkeley, but the third is left at the plantation for the guarding of the paper you must somehow secure; but how to do it — I have no advice to give. Alas, 't is so easy to say 'must' — so hard to show how!"

"Sure 't is enough for one man to carry the whole scheme of this war in his head without burdening his mind with every trifle. Leave these to us smaller men. I will set off this very night, and ride from Gloucester Court House here to the shore of the York River, where I do know a man, not over trusty, but he may serve my turn, for he will ferry me across; and thereafter I must trust to fate and my mother wit to help me out."

"This very night say you? Have ye forgot that 't is Friday?" asked Bacon, who despite his reason shared the superstition of his age.

"All the better," answered Fairfax, lightly. "I will try how unlucky a day I can make it for Berkeley; and methinks when he finds his hand forced in this fashion he will wear dust and ashes on his head as befits a fast-day. Now fare you well, General, and expect me not till ye do see me."

"Farewell, lad, and God be wi' ye!"

It was near morning when a little boat put out from shore on the York River. After it swam a horse, whose head struggled bravely through the waves. The boat made its way swiftly enough across the open river; but as it neared the shore it moved more slowly, like a live creature groping its way, till at last its keel grated on the sandy beach where the waters of Queen's Creek join the wider and deeper tide of the York River.

As the boat touched land, Bryan Fairfax sprang ashore, and by dint of tugging at the rope about his mare's head brought her up safe and sound though shivering. Snatching a rag of rough wool which lay in the bottom of the boat, he rubbed her down briskly, saying softly in her ear: "Bravely done, my Peggy! Ye shall have a scarlet saddle-cloth and a silver bridle chain in honor of your long swim this night, if we come safely out of this business, which, betwixt you and me, Peggy, is a ticklish one. Ay, my beauty, arch your neck and paw the ground with pride! Ye are like the rest of the females, — mightily elated with the prospect of new gauds and finery."

"Now, good Master Boatman," he added, turning toward the one who had ferried him over, and who now stood in the stern of his boat, a shadowy figure against the growing dawn, "here's a bit o' silver for you, and mind ye keep a still tongue in your head or Bacon will find means to still it for you. Remember, ye are to be at this same spot to-morrow night, or next morning rather, in the dark o' the moon. Hide your boat and yourself under the shadow of these cypress trees, and bide quiet till you hear me whistle thrice."

A Trader.

"Ay, sir. I'll not fail," answered the boatman, as coming forward he buried his oar in the sand and leaned upon it as he shoved the skiff back into deep water.

Fairfax stood alone, watching the ripples part and close again in the wake of the retreating boat. He shivered a little in the chill morning air, drew his cloak closer about him, and kicked idly at a stone which lay beside his foot. The sun rose round and red across the river. Still he stood there, his eyes cast down as if the answer to his thoughts might be found in the broken shells or the heavy overhanging grasses which fringed the beach. At length he said to himself: "Verily necessity is not only the mother but the whole family of invention. I must seek some disguise, — but what? My sword first of all must be buried, so off with it and under this stone. Now if I do rub my skin brown with the juice of yonder berries, and dust my hat, and tear my breeches, and turn my coat inside out, I may perchance trust to passing for some indented servant who hath strayed from his master."

So saying he stooped, and, searching in the deep grass for the brown berries, he pulled them, and rubbed their juices on face, hands, and arms till he was darkened almost past recognition by his oldest friend. So closely was he occupied that his ear, usually swift as an Indian's at catching at any sound, failed to take in the approach of a horse and rider till they were close upon him.

"Goot morning, stranger!" said the rider. "Gan ye dell me if dere iss any ford or ferry so dat me and mein horse gan gome by de oder side off diss riffer?"

It was with infinite relief that Fairfax noted the accent. The utterance was thicker than any known in Virginia, and the rolling of the words in the mouth like a bit of Dutch cheese, too large either to swallow or spew out, bespoke the dweller by the Kill Van Kull or on the banks of the Hudson. Looking up, Fairfax found that the voice had not deceived him. The coat was longer and less natty than that in vogue among the cavaliers, the hat plainer and broader in the brim, and the riding-boots of a clumsier make. Nor was the costume all. The load bound upon the horse told of itself that this was some trader from Dutch New York bent on selling his wares among the unthrifty Southerners to a greater profit than he could hope to do among his close-fisted brethren nearer home. As Fairfax looked at him a light flashed into the dark corners of his mind.

"Ye will find no ferry here," he answered, "and

for a ford ye must seek many a mile farther up the river, and even there ye will find it so deep that no horse loaded as yours is could make land save at the bottom. Now, if you can unbind that bundle and leave it behind —"

"Leaf de boondle behint, is it? Goot Gott! I radder stay behint myself und sent de boondle ofer. Don you see I must sell dese tings! For dat am I gome into dis defflish gountry vot got no roads, no ferries, no cheese, no ganals, no nodding."

"Then you would like to get rid of your wares and this devilish country together, and as speedily as possible, and get you back to your long pipe and mug of beer and your Katrina — hein?" said Fairfax, throwing a droll imitation of the Dutchman's accent into the last word.

"Glat!" cried the trader, his eyes bulging and rolling heavenward till nothing but the yellow whites could be seen. "But you do but make sport off me!"

"Sport? Not at all. I do be much in earnest, as you shall shortly learn. What if I should offer to buy your whole stock here and now, so that you could ford the river with a light load and a heavy purse?"

The stranger looked at him out of his dull blue

eyes, keen enough to suspect a cheat, but not keen enough to detect it. "Nay," said Fairfax, answering the look as though he had spoken. "'T is neither jest nor fraud. The truth is, I have long wished to set up in some trade, but unluckily, my habit is so fine that none will hire me for service, believing I have run away with my master's clothing, and none would buy of a pedler in a velvet coat and breeches. Now, what say you to trading with me all in all, — save for the horse, which I would not exchange for any nag living. But my trimmed, rich coat against your baggy, plain one — my velvet breeches against your homespun — my plumed hat against your stiff, broad brim? Think, man, how the folk along the Harlem will stare their eyes out at your rich attire!"

The trader's eyes sparkled; but in an instant he recollected himself. "But how goes it about de goots?" he asked, as one who had long ago learned to turn too fair a bargain to the sun, and to look twice for the holes in cheap cloth.

"Ah — the goods — to be sure," said Fairfax slowly, bethinking himself that he might lose all by showing over-much eagerness. "Now I come to scan them more closely, I see they are worn, and belike the furs already stink so that none will buy. The furs are ill cured, I should guess, the gilt chains are very brass, the tabby velvet hath no sheen, and, in short, methinks I was too hasty in my offer, so go your way and I will go mine. I give you good day!"

The bait took. As Fairfax grew cool the trader grew hot for the bargain. "Poof," he answered, "vat you call vorn iss vere de fur iss so dick it press itself down. Mein Gott, dey iss de best furs on de goast, und de gloth und de chains iss fine. Gome, now, vot you gif for dem?"

"No, no, you old coon," thought Fairfax, "you'll get no offer out of me," — then aloud — "Oh, I don't know that I fancy them at all; but figure up the cost, and I may consider of the matter."

"Vell, den," quoth the Dutchman, "it take me dree mont to puy dese skins off de nadives, und I risk my life besides. Den I must gound de vear und dear on my horse."

"Oh, yes, yes, I know," broke in Fairfax, growing impatient; "count in at thrippence your wife's grief at parting, and add sixpence for the baby's croup caught in crying after you. But an we come not to terms within five seconds, the business is off."

The Dutchman, accustomed to the leisurely ways of Manhattan, where the pleasures of bargaining were extended over hours, if not days, opened his mouth wide with astonishment; but seeing his chance in danger of slipping through his fingers, he pulled his faculties together with a desperate effort, and drawing forth from the wide pocket of his coat a note-book, he fell to figuring the actual cost of the furs; then he hastily doubled the amount and said, "Vell, shoost to get done vid dis goundry I lets you haf de lot at fifty grouns."

"Fifty crowns! Why, man, there is not so much gold in York County. Do you take me for some Mynherr with an iron pot full of money under his brick floor? No, no! You sure have been scant time in Virginia, else ye would have learned that here we pay our debts, when we pay them at all, not in crowns, but in pounds, and pounds of tobacco at that. Now, which will ye have, my draft on General Bacon at Gloucester Court House yonder for a thousand pounds of tobacco, or these five gold pieces, bright and new as the pewter in a Harlem cottage?" With a keen instinctive knowledge of human nature in general, and Dutch nature in particular, Fairfax drew forth the gold as he spoke and jingled it in his hand. The jingle and the glitter represented an alluring concrete wealth not to be resisted.

"Take id all den," cried the trader. "You haf goot drading bloot in your veins, und if effer you gomes to Nieuw Amsterdam (vot dey calls New York now), ve beads all de men from de old Fort to de Bowery."

Thanking the stranger for so fair an opening in the future and so fair a bargain for the present, Fairfax lost no time in beginning to strip, and in short order found himself arrayed in the loose flapping coat, wide hat, and loose-fitting boots of the Dutch trader, with whose help he shifted the saddles on the horses. When the haughty thoroughbred, Peggy, first felt the heavy load on her back, she shied, and pranced, and rubbed against a tree, striving to scrape off the hated burden; and when she could not, she but curveted the more, as if in protest against the hardship, for a horse of her pedigree, of being put to such plebeian labors.

Her master succeeded in soothing her somewhat with the magnetism of his voice; but when he stood before her, holding out a bunch of sweet ferns, she looked askance at him, planted her fore feet, and pulled away as from a stranger.

"Good," said Fairfax, "'t is the first tribute to the completeness of my transformation. From horses and children — very young children — you may hope to learn the truth. Now, Master Dutchman," he added, turning to the trader who stood there so ill at ease in his new finery, and so comical a burlesque of the recent wearer of the garb that Fairfax was nigh bursting with laughter as he looked on him, "before we part perhaps you will do me the honor to tell me your name."

The Dutchman looked at him out of the corner of his eye as one loath to part with even a piece of information which was not in the bargain, but at length vouchsafed the answer that he was called Van der Stosch.

"Well, then, Mynherr Van der Stosch," cried Fairfax, gayly, "I bid you good day, and I promise you I will not forget your kind offer of furthering my fortunes if ever I come to New Amsterdam. Now, to make you unhappy, let me whisper in your ear before we part that I know a market for these skins where I can sell them at such a profit as will turn you yellow with envy when I bring you the tidings!"

So saying, Fairfax rode off laughing, and leaving the trader standing by the shore uncertain whether he had made a fool of his companion or himself.

CHAPTER VI.

MONTAGUE AND CAPULET.

"O Romeo, Romeo! wherefore art thou Romeo?"

SO pleased was Fairfax with this fair beginning to his enterprise that he rode along in higher spirits than had blessed him in many days. Now he trolled snatches of song, now boylike he stopped to call a quail by a mocking note that matched its own, and laughed to see the eager questioning eye which met his as the bird looked up and down the road in search of its missing mate.

His mind wandered idly from theme to theme. He recalled Bacon's words uttered on the day of the battle at Green Spring, and was sad for a moment; but then, with the happy shortsightedness of youth, dismissed them lightly as the passing whim of a momentary depression. At length he returned to the thoughts in which his mind steeped itself by night and by day, — thoughts of Penelope Payne, of the rosemary which she had worn at her breast, and which he might have picked up and did not (fool that he was!), — of the kindness in her eyes when she said: "Be my friend!" — of the glory about her head as she leaned from the window.

Suddenly the hot blood mounted from his heart to his temples, and he gave a sort of gasp, — and why? All because he remembered on the instant that Rosemary Hall stood at the head of this creek along which his road was winding. 'T would be but five miles out of his course at the most, and he desired not to reach the Boynton plantation till nightfall. Oh, to see her again, to look upon her once more, though himself unseen, unrecognized, unthought of ! — that were happiness indeed to set a man's brain reeling.

In the wild turmoil of his new-born eagerness, he struck his spurs so deep into poor Peggy's side that the astonished beast gave a leap that was like to land her rider in the ditch by the roadside; but he heeded her protest not a whit.

"I have it!" he cried aloud. "The letter I did write three nights since, when I could get no sleep for thinking of her, is among the papers in my wallet. I will give it into her hand by stealth, saying one in Bacon's camp where I did stop bade me carry it, as my road lay this way."

Throwing the reins upon his horse's neck, he drew it forth and read as he ambled along, though the paper was now and then nearly jerked from his fingers by the roughness of the road.

"Sweetest friend or dearest foe!" (so it ran) "I have been so tormented with thoughts of thee since ever we did meet and part yonder at Green Spring, that human nature can bear it no longer. If thou dost not send me some word or token to tell me that thou too hast sometimes wasted a thought on me, I shall —" (Here certain words were erased.) "Tell me not," the letter continued, "that my love is too sudden, that swift come is swift gone, or any such thing, for I tell thee this affection is so woven in the very tissues of my soul as not death itself shall be able to separate it and me. But for thee I grant the time has been o'er brief for me to cherish hope that thou couldst have learned to love me, even hadst thou had no enmity to be conquered in thine heart. Say only that thou dost no longer hate and I am satisfied — no, never believe it, — for neither that nor much more will content my greedy heart, — yet say '*wait and hope!*' and for the present I will ask no more. Three words, — three little words, — and in exchange I offer thee a heart full of love and devotion. Good-bye, my friend. Shall I not dare some day, when this unhappy strife is ended, to speak those dearest words, — my love, *my wife?*"

Having finished reading over his letter, Fairfax looked about for some means of sealing it. His eye lighted on the gum oozing in a glittering sticky stream from the bark of the Norway pine. Dismounting, he took out his knife, and hacking off a great drop, he made from it a rude fastening for the folded sheet. This done, he once more climbed into his saddle and urged Peggy into a brisk trot, to make up for lost time. Before an hour had passed the walls of Rosemary rose before his eyes.

At the gate he alighted and took his horse by the bridle, as was the custom amongst pedlers when approaching a house, and, his heart beating like a trip-hammer, he drew near the porch. When he had come within a few yards he lifted up his eyes and they fell upon — *Col. Theophilus Payne.*

How did Bryan Fairfax feel? Much, I fancy, as Romeo would have felt if Signor Capulet had thrust his head forth from Juliet's balcony when the young Montague's foot was on the highest round of the midnight rope-ladder: much as Leander might have felt had he seen Hero's father waiting to help him ashore on the unfriendly banks of the Hellespont.

Montague and Capulet.

Indeed, it would be idle to try to describe the sensations of Fairfax, — for he himself scarcely comprehended them, so overcome was he by the shock of surprise, while, mingled with his emotion came for the first time a realizing sense that to gain a private end he had imperilled the trust confided in him. How could he hope a second time to be forgiven? Even his love, which but an hour since had seemed to fill the whole heaven of his life from zenith to horizon, now shrank into a small matter in comparison with the great public cause. All this flashed through his mind as swiftly as memories throng past the mental vision of a drowning man. But he found himself compelled to gather all his faculties to meet the present crisis.

Colonel Payne's first words gave him great comfort and relief in the complete lack of recognition that they betrayed. It was evident that no shadow of suspicion had crossed his mind, no connection of this wayfarer with the young officer who had ridden into Jamestown a month ago, bearing messages from the rebel camp.

"How now, my good man?" began the Colonel, in the friendly tone of easy patronage befitting a gentleman addressing an inferior. "These be troublous times for a poor pedler to be wandering about the country with his wares. By your dusty garments and your ungroomed horse I judge ye have travelled far, and by your fair hair and swarthy skin I do suspect that ye be a Hollander from the colony of New Netherland. Is 't not so?"

Strange to say, Fairfax was wholly taken aback by this sudden question. It had not dawned upon his mind that he must carry out the rôle of Dutchman, and that speech and manner must match with boots and breeches. But now he realized that being in deep water he must strike out or sink; so, though painfully aware that his accent fitted him as ill as his coat, he assented in broken English to the Colonel's question.

"I fear you have come to the wrong market, for we in Virginia are too poor now to buy aught but necessaries. What is your name?"

Again Fairfax gasped, and again he snatched at the nearest lie. "Van der Stosch," he answered, taking off his hat, but replacing it instantly in the fear that the dye might have escaped his forehead.

"Well, Master Van der Stosch, you must be mightily dull, even for a Dutchman, an ye have not learned in the course of your travels that we have a rebellion on our hands here in Virginia; and war, you must know, eats up luxuries faster than a cat laps milk."

Fairfax inquired innocently if the Indians were making trouble once more. "Pretty well!" thought he. "I am lying with a smoother and more tripping tongue. These confounded *v*'s and *w*'s do more confuse me than the prevarication."

"Nay, man," answered the Colonel, gravely, "'t is more than any outbreak of Indians. 'T is what is called a civil war, though why it should be so named I could never guess; for sure the world ne'er looked on anything more uncivilized than this warring betwixt brethren."

Fairfax felt the heart within him so choked that he dared not trust himself to speak for a moment; and while he hesitated he heard a light, lilting voice in the hallway, caught sight of a flash of white drapery on the stair, and an instant later beheld a pair of bright eyes peeping over Colonel Payne's broad shoulders, which well-nigh filled the entrance.

"Oh, naught save furs and finery!" exclaimed Penelope, scanning the load of skins to which Fairfax had turned for occupation, hoping to hide his trembling. "I did hope the man had pewter, or at least wooden ware for sale, since we do be mightily in need thereof."

"Come out, my darling, my rose, my sunshine!" called Colonel Payne, showering pet names as though no *one* could hold the fulness of his tenderness, and his face lighting up as if a ray of actual sunshine had crossed it. "Come out and talk with this poor fellow, who I fear is hugely disappointed to be told that we Virginians have no money to spend on furs and such like luxuries. I for one am well content with bare floors. Still, for thy bedside in the winter-time I own I would fain have just such a carpet as that brown skin yonder."

"Nay, nay, father mine! You must not strive to spoil me thus. It were ill befitting that I should be wrapped in luxury when all Virginia goeth bare of comforts and even necessaries."

"Methinks," said the Colonel, smiling and stroking tenderly the little hand laid in his own, "'t is spoke but as I should look to hear my daughter speak, and my softness is rebuked of her wisdom. It is, as you say, no time to consider ourselves. Now if it were his horse the man was wishing to sell, I might think on 't; for Berkeley do be grievously in want of transports, and I have had no good horse since Buck was shot under me at Green Spring."

"Ay, father; and sorely have I grieved over poor Buck, yet withal did more rejoice for your escape, of the which and your rescue by the timely help of that young officer, Bryan Fairfax, I could hear you tell forever and never weary. Even for the flesh-wound I could be glad, since it gained you this leave of absence to come home and be tended by mother and me. Poor mamma! Methinks since those days in the camp she do fade and pine, for all I strive to feed and cheer her."

The Colonel raised his hand and brushed away a tear. "Come, come," he said, "this will never do. Say no more, lest ye unman me quite. Let us talk about the horse. Penelope, ye have as good an eye for horse-flesh as any jockey in York County. Look close at this black mare and tell me what ye think of her, for by my troth she looks to me a horse of such value that I be more than half inclined to the belief that the pedler hath stole her."

With this Penelope sprang lightly down the steps, her father tarrying to find his hat. Fairfax turned to look upon her, but a sort of mist gathered before his eyes, and he seemed to see some white angel just poised ready for flight. The angel, however, had a shrewd little head of her own, quite awake to earthly matters, and a keen eye, which now swept over the horse swiftly, taking account of all its points, — the free floating mane, the slim, sinewy legs, the barrel tapering toward the haunches, the delicate, almost transparent ears, the backward-turning, fiery eye. Penelope puckered her pretty forehead in thought. Surely — surely she had seen all these somewhere before. In sooth Peggy was a horse once seen not soon to be forgot; for there was not her like in the whole of tide-water Virginia.

At length the girl opened her lips to speak; then swift as lightning her eyes rose from the horse to the master. Fairfax abandoned hope as he caught that glance, so full was it of comprehension, of detection, of disdain. Yet he threw her back a look as haughty and uncompromising as her own, — a look which said as plain as words could have spoken, "I am at your mercy; but I ask no favor." Whilst Penelope stood with parted lips, uncertain whether to speak or to keep silence, her father's voice broke the pause, saying:

"What think ye? is it not a fine creature?"

"Yea," answered the girl, like one in a daze.

"Well, then, my little jockey, I will leave thee to chaffer with the trader whiles I go in and order a mug of ale and a trencher of bread set out in the kitchen; for I warrant both man and horse will be the better for a good meal." So saying, the Colonel turned his back, ascended the steps, and entered the wide, hospitable hall.

"Well, sir," broke out Mistress Payne, "what have ye to say for yourself why I should not denounce you to my father for the spy ye are?"

"I have naught to say, Mistress Payne," answered Fairfax, stonily calm. "Denounce me when and where and to whom ye will, yet am I not come as a spy to Rosemary."

"Indeed!" exclaimed the girl, with irony in the curve of her lip and eyebrow. "Perchance ye would have me believe you what your wares and habit proclaim, — a simple tradesman come all the way from New Amsterdam selling furs along the road. Let me see — I think I heard you tell my father your name was Van der Stosch — well, then, Mr. Van der Stosch, I would have you know I do despise you; ay, and I do despise myself well-nigh as much when I remember how near I was once to feeling — " Fairfax could hear his heart beat while she paused — "yes," she continued, swallowing hard, "to feeling *friendship* for one who called himself Bryan Fairfax, — though perchance that too was but a name assumed to meet the purpose of the hour."

"Say no more, Mistress Payne!" burst forth Fairfax, in a flame of rage and mortified pride and wounded love; "ye have already said enough to make me feel bitter shame that I was so weak as to imperil business of mighty moment for one glimpse of thee and the chance of a touch of those fingers of thine. Fool that I was! 't was for that I have been riding since early dawn, 't was for that I did think to give this letter into your little hand. Yes, look at me again with scorn in that curling lip; it is the best cure for my fool's passion, which I do swear to stamp out as I now stamp on its avowal."

With this Fairfax drew forth from his breast the letter which held the outpourings of his love, and with a quick movement he tore it in twain and would have cast it under his heel; but Penelope's hand stayed him, and Penelope's fingers grasped the torn pieces of paper. "Give me the letter," she said, speaking low and quick.

Fairfax yielded the fragments to her grasp, and as he did so he felt the anger fading fast. "Now," said she, "look in my eyes, and swear if ye can that you came to Rosemary not to plot harm and dark designs against my kith and kin, but solely and only as ye did say but now, to look on my face and hear my voice."

"Penelope," answered Fairfax, coming a step nearer, "I swear I could as soon desire injury to myself as to thee or those whom thou dost love. But of a truth when thou dost bid me look into thine eyes, thou dost forefend my thoughts from dwelling on aught else but just my great love for thee, — a love deeper and stronger than all the floods of wrath and bitterness which do rage around us. Say, sweetheart, do my words find no echo in thine own soul?"

"Oh," cried the girl, as one whose heart is shaken by a gust of passion too strong for her and who feels her foothold losing its grasp, "ask me no such question — I know not how to answer — wert thou not a rebel — but no — already for thy sake I have deceived my father — ah, it makes me hate myself to think on 't. Yea, and it makes me hate thee too."

Fairfax staggered as if a blow had struck him. "Nay — I meant it not!" cried poor Penelope, well-nigh distraught. "But make haste to get away from here lest thou be seized and shot, — and then what were my life worth?"

"Ah, Penelope, say those words once more!"

"No, of a truth I know not what I say; but get thee gone and I will explain thy going somehow to my father — more deceiving — alas, lies do come thick and fast to my lips which till now have scorned them."

"Penelope, I will stay or go, or whatsoever you do bid me, but speak one word before I go — say only 'hope'!"

"Nay, not a single word will I speak, — at least not now. Yet I would not have thee wholly despair. Thou shalt shortly hear from me, — so much I promise; but for the purport of the message I do promise thee naught. Farewell! Rebel as thou art, my heart is little better than a rebel too. Farewell!"

CHAPTER VII.

THE KING'S COMMISSION.

Pereat qui me lacessit.

SO shaken was the mind of Fairfax by the mingled emotions which had been stirred within him during his visit to Rosemary Hall, that when he took the highroad again he went forward in a daze. Like a child with the petals of a daisy, he repeated over and over the refrain, — "She loves me — she loves me not — she loves me — not." Monotonous indeed to the cool bystander, but to the anxious heart torn by alternating hopes and fears, agonies and expectations, the whirlwind were a dead calm in comparison.

Morning drew on to noon and noon to evening. Fairfax had a vague recollection of having paused at the hottest height of the sun to drink by a brook and eat of the bread and meat which he had taken good care to transfer to the Dutchman's wallet. Save for this remembrance of eating and drinking he seemed to himself to have been riding all day in a trance, like Saint Bernard by the side of his Swiss lake.

The rays of the setting sun were shining long and level on the road, and lighting up the under side of the boughs of the sombre pines which skirted the shores of the Chickahominy River, when the broad open gate and stone posts of the Boynton plantation rose before Fairfax and told him that his journey was accomplished, and that the decisive hour of success or failure was close at hand.

Dismounting, he eased Peggy of her load and tethered her to a tree, — for he was too good a horseman to allow her to partake of food or water till she had rested, — and he, having washed off the dust of travel, and with it the stain of the berries from his face and hands, stretched himself out on the bank by her side, working out as best he could his plans for the securing of that which he had come to seek. At length, rising from the ground, he drew forth a small sack of oats from the saddle-bag and tied it over Peggy's nose, saying as he did so, "There may be work for you this night, my girl, and oats to a horse are like toddy to a man, and do lift the heart over many a hard bit of road; therefore will I feed thee myself, and trust to no

The King's Commission.

lazy hostler, who may be filling thy belly with hay, and giving thee colic with over-cold water when thou art hot. I tell thee, Peggy, much of what men call good luck lies in a man's trusting to it as little as may be."

When the mare had finished her supper, nosing eagerly for the last grain hid in the cracks of the seaming in the bag, Fairfax took the bridle over his arm and drew near the open gate. As he turned from the highway (or what passed in Virginia for a highway, which was little more than a track marked by the felling of a few trees and the blazing of a few more) into the private road within sight of a brick house, two mastiffs came dashing down the drive with a barking which laid Peggy's ears back flat against her head and set her to walking circus fashion on her hind legs; but ere the dogs had come half way, a sharp whistle sounded from the porch, and a deep, gruff voice called: " Here, Bruno! Here, Catnip! Back, you hell-hounds — damn you: I'll have you whipped till the blood runs, an ye rush out like that again unbidden!"

The dogs thus rudely recalled showed the humanness of their nature by their worship of power. They cringed back to the feet of their master and fell to licking his hands; while he, having vented his wrath, turned amiable, patted them on the head, and, holding each by the collar, moved between them down the road to meet the new-comer.

"Cloth and chains and silks and furs for sale, eh!" said he, peering through the gathering dusk at the pedler and his load. "Well, I am in want of no such lollipops, so ye may as well move on. I wonder not that my dogs were fain to fall on you, for ye are an outlandish figure enough,—a mongrel, I should say, a cross twixt Dutch and English. Which are ye, anyway?"

Fairfax's morning experience warned him not to attempt again the assuming of a strange tongue wherein he ran such risk of detection, especially should any by chance offer to hold converse with him in his adopted language; therefore, putting on a bold and easy manner, he made answer: "I am as good an Englishman as you, if I do chance to hail from a Dutch colony; but I would have you know my wares are for sale but not my history, and of a surety neither the one nor the other is to be given away, nor yet to be worried out of me by you and those infernal dogs of yours. Now a bit of supper, and something to wash it down withal, were more to the purpose, and methinks would comport better with the tales I have heard of Virginia hospitality."

"Come in, then," cried Boynton, with a round, mouth-filling oath. "My kinsman, the master of this house, were he at home, would send you out for bit and sup with the servants, for he do build much on his blue blood, and is for drawing the line mighty straight 'twixt the gentry and such as you, and his lady none the less; but she is fled to Accomac, and he gone to join Berkeley, so I am master for the nonce, and having been brought up as 't were in a tavern, if I did chance to be born in a mansion, I have had opportunity to learn that blue blood runs monstrous slow, and that Bill and Sam and Moll and Sue at the ordinary are better company than Ma'am Fine-airs and Master Bagwig at the Hall, — besides, now I am forbid to leave the plantation, I must consort with such as come to me, or else gnaw my heart out here alone."

"Tough eating, methinks," answered Fairfax; then seeing his words like to give offence to one who had heavy humor enough to crack a jest but not sharpness enough to get at the meat in that of another, as is the wont of those who tarry too much at home, he made haste to add, "I have gnawed mine so oft in sheer loneliness that I know the taste well, and do dislike it much."

"Come in, then," cried the host, with more heartiness than he had yet shown, — "come in and bide the night with me, and we will rub loneliness as calves rub noses in the pasture."

Pleased with his own wit, Boynton turned, still chuckling; and as he went before him Fairfax had opportunity to mark the gigantic height and breadth which had given him the name by which he was known far and wide, of "Big Boynton." When he reached the steps the giant thundered out a call for the hostler in a voice which suited well with his frame, and which straightway brought four black boys, tumbling over each other's heels in their eagerness to be first.

"Take this man's mare!" ordered the master of the house, "and look to her well, for I have not a better one in the stable. Rub her down, let her stand an hour, and then give her supper."

"I thank you," answered Fairfax, "but she was fed some distance back,—I try always to deal fairly by my horse if I have to pinch my own belly to do it. Sponge out her mouth," he added, turning to the stable boy, "and let her stand. I will come out myself after supper to see to her; for she and I have wandered about the world together so long that she would never close an eye an I came not to bid her good night."

"So be it," said his host. "I think the more of a man who looks after his own beast; I do the like myself." To do as he did was to approach the only standard of perfection Boynton had ever set up. The stranger was growing in favor moment by moment.

The candles were lighted in the dark dining-room, to which he led the way. Their yellow rays shone on a great mug of Delft ware, and danced on the shining circle of the solitary pewter plate which stood at the head of the table. When Boynton saw it his brow clouded like that of a spoiled, angry child, who expects his wishes understood and attended to without his taking the trouble to make them known.

"How's this?" he growled. "D'ye expect two men to eat like dogs, — off the one plate?"

The servant made answer timidly that the stranger's supper was set out in the kitchen.

"Fool!" shouted his master. "Think ye I will waste so good a chance to catch news of all that is stirring in the great world, while you black devils stretch your ears to take all in by the kitchen fire? Fetch another plate, I say, and another noggin, and if you care for your carcass be quick about it!"

Boynton brought down his fist with a resounding whack, which set the plate spinning on the table and sent the man even more hurriedly to the pantry, whence he came out a moment later bearing plate and mug, together with a steel knife and a two-tined fork.

"Fall to!" cried Boynton. "Take a fork and eat like a gentleman for once."

To a man who had been all day in the saddle in the keen autumn air there ordinarily might have needed little bidding to persuade him to help himself from the platter of cold meat, the great trencher of bread, the smoking bacon, and the bowl of hominy; but Fairfax could not brook the thought of breaking bread with the man he had come to rob, though 't was of something not rightfully his; and for all he made great parade of helping himself bountifully, little passed his lips, and that little went near to choking him. But Boynton was too absorbed in the enjoyment of his own meal, whereof he partook till the veins swelled in his forehead, to note the abstinence of his companion. When he had devoured a goodly share of all set before him, he pushed away the plate, bade the servants set on more wine, and then leave the room and plague him no more that night, which, according well with their sleepy wishes, they accepted as permission to be off to their quarters and abed.

"Oh, and I say," called the master after them, "bid Sam leave the stable door open, that the trader may look after his horse ere he go to bed."

"Ay, and tie up the dogs in their kennel, if it please you," added Fairfax, "for I have no taste for such a greeting as I did receive this afternoon."

"Ay," said Boynton, "off to the quarters with the dogs! And now," he added, turning toward Fairfax, "try your hand at the noggin, and we two will show our strength at a drinking bout wherein I have never yet met my match."

Fairfax felt that his opportunity had come. Could he but lay this guardian under the table, he might prosecute his search undisturbed. "But," thought he, "while my head is as steady as the next man's, I do count myself no match for this giant, whose looks belie him if he was not suckled on Madeira in place of milk."

Boynton filled both noggins from the huge pewter flagon which stood by his elbow, and raising his mug to his mouth drained it at a single gulp, then wiped his lips with the back of his brawny hand, and setting the noggin down hard enough to have broken a daintier vessel in a thousand fragments, he cried out, "Ha! I am one noggin to the good already, for you have scarce dipped your nose in yours."

"Ay, mark yourself down one. I acknowledge

myself so deep in your debt," answered Fairfax, gayly; while to himself he said, "Methinks he can not hold out long at this pace, for drinking is like driving,—a swift start makes a poor ending."

"'T is a huge, noble house, this of yours," he continued aloud, letting his eye roam in leisurely fashion about the room. "We see little of such splendor north of the Delaware. Our gambrel roofs do cover comfort but not luxury."

"No, no," answered Big Boynton, with the smile of one who counts himself and his belongings far above all comparison with the world outside his own plantations. "Of course there be no province like Virginia; but for the matter o' that, ye will not find many mansions in the length and breadth of the Old Dominion so fine as this."

"I do credit it well. Troth it must have seven or eight rooms."

"Seven or eight, man! I would have you know it hath *thirteen*, besides the offices set off by themselves in other buildings." Here the giant paused, and poured out another nogginful of the liquor with a triumphant wink at Fairfax, who took pains to open wide his mouth and eyes in amazement, exclaiming, "Why, it were a mansion fit for the Duke of York, in whose honor our colony of New Netherland is new named. I remember me once of being taken through his palace in London, and 't was so full of passages and secret closets a man might have lain hid therein for fifty years and none suspicioned him. I suppose many great houses be like that, for I was told while Charles was over the water some of his father's crown jewels lay under Oliver's big nose in the very closet where he was wont to say his canting, long-winded prayers. By the way, how runs that motto carved on the mantel-breast behind you?"

Boynton twisted himself about heavily in his chair; and while his back was turned, Fairfax deftly upset the contents of his noggin under the table. "Ah ha!" thought he, "'t was not for naught I did read in my youth the tale of Jack and how he overcame the giant." Then aloud, "Fill me another noggin, mine host, and let me see thee take of that one of thine."

As Boynton drank, Fairfax could see that a slight film was gathering over his eyes, his cheek was flushing, his utterance growing thicker, and his confidences more garrulous.

"That motto," said he, "is not for ignorant fellows like you to read. It is writ in Latin, which being a dead language this thousand years, is apt to stink when 't is dug up, and therefore have I let it more or less alone myself, though I had as much schooling as becomes the son of a Virginia gentleman, — which, between me and you and yonder post, is little enough. But for this motto, being that of our house, I made out to decipher and learned it by heart, and faith 't is a good one, — '*Pereat qui me lacessit;*' that means, He that harms a Boynton is as good as a dead man."

"So," said Fairfax, "it is well to warn all comers who would trespass by thus printing of their fate before their eyes." Boynton looked at him close to make sure if he were in jest; but Fairfax's face was as solemn as a tombstone.

"As for what ye were saying of Charles," quoth Boynton, lying back in his chair, "I do think him after all a fool for his pains. 'Set a man to nosing round like a ferret,' say I, 'and ye put him on the scent at once for some secret.' Now if I had aught to hide, — which were little likely in this poor country, where all the wealth is underground, — but if any shrewd man had such a treasure, he'd better set it somewhere in easy reach, just about a room in plain sight perchance."

Fairfax closed his eyes lest the light therein should betray him. "Ay," said he, stretching his arms above his head and yawning wide enough to show his back teeth, "ye are a wise man, master; 't is a pity there is so little treasure here to try your craft on: we in New Netherland have more need of something to hide than of a hiding-place. The squirrels are the only misers among us, — but I am growing so heavy with sleep that I must soon crave your permission to retire vanquished from our drinking bout with the confession that ye are the valiantest man at both trencher and noggin I did e'er encounter; yet before I go I would fain see you drain one more mug, that I may have the larger tale to tell when I am returned home."

Pleased to receive the palm for the noble virtues of gluttony and wine-bibbing, Boynton filled his noggin, drank deep, and held it upside down to prove that the last drop was gone; but even as he did so, the red eyelids closed, the head fell heavily forward on his breast, and the drunken snore told that the liquor had done its work.

The faculties of Fairfax, on the contrary, were alert. "No time to lose," thought he. "Let me consider — an open place — that might be in this very room, — under the hearth? No, the dullest thief would search there first. Perchance there openeth a cupboard behind that portrait of the old gentleman whose ruffles swell out like a pouter pigeon. Methinks he smiles a little as the fire plays on his face. Come on, then, Sir Whatever

Your Name; stiff as you look you shall move, I swear, and give me a chance to see what you cover!"

He rose cautiously and turned the Boynton ancestor to the wall; but no paper was tucked into the corner of the frame. He turned to the wainscot and tapped it with his knuckle; but the joinings were close, and no crack or crevice gave evidence of any hiding-place within. He stooped and felt along the under-side of every chair-seat; except for the roughness of the wood the two sides were alike. He flung open the door of the cupboard; every shelf was bare. Then a sudden frenzy of impotent rage seized him. To be so near success and yet to fail,—oh, it was intolerable! But it was not in the nature of a Fairfax to dwell long on the idea of failure. He clung to his purpose with the tenacity of a bull-dog. The commission he had come to seek, and the commission he must have,—yes, if he hired himself out as a servant to the lump of clay in yonder chair. He would dog his footsteps, live with him by day and night, share his dull company, bear his coarse abuse and coarser familiarity,—but that commission he *would* have.

The Dutch clock which hung high upon the wall struck the hour of half-past eleven. His heart in his mouth, Fairfax waited to see if its tone disturbed the sleeper; but Boynton only turned drowsily in his chair, threw back his head, and snored the louder. "First of all," thought Fairfax, "we must stop that. The next stroke will be on the hour of midnight, which may fall in the middle of my search, and I dare not trust twelve strokes even on ear as dead in drunkenness as his." As Fairfax looked anxiously at the face of the clock, the jolly round Dutch moon in one corner seemed to be smiling in derision of his plight; but as he looked, suddenly his gaze grew fixed, — not by that stolid painted countenance, but by something in the opposite corner, where a round hole of the size of a bull's eye had been rudely cut out, and was filled by a figured red disk, which ordinarily would have attracted no attention, save as some bright-colored decoration set in to balance the apple-cheeked moon; but now, to the heated fancy of Fairfax it took on the semblance of a state seal. Oh, could it be that fortune, in very raillery at his vaunted cunning, had thrust this treasure into his hand as into that of one too dull to find it for himself! Yes, he saw it all now. No better hiding-place could be devised; for here a paper tucked away in the top of the clock, yet peeping out at this hole, was always under the eye of its guardian. Verily this Boynton was not the stupid oaf he had seemed, or else he — Fairfax — was the duller of the two.

Stretching up his arm, Fairfax first of all made haste to stay the pendulum, fearing lest the very ticking should awaken the sleeper at the critical moment. Then climbing upon a chair he reached over the high carved top with its brass balls, and, grasping the paper, drew it forth with trembling hand. As he opened it, all doubts ceased, for there was the name of Nathaniel Bacon written in a clerkly hand, and a great Charles R. sprawled at the foot of the page.

Thrusting the precious paper into his bosom, Fairfax drew off his boots and stole with noiseless foot-fall across the floor. As he went, his eye fell by chance upon the motto on the mantel-breast: "*Pereat qui me lacessit.*" In his exultation he shook his boots first at it, then at the portrait on the wall, as if bidding defiance to the whole house of Boynton. From the dining-room he passed into the saloon, unlighted save by the moon, which, however, shone brightly enough through the window to show him the way to the door. To his joy he found it unlocked; but as he stirred the handle it creaked, and Fairfax started with such an alarm as shook the hearts of Christian and

Hopeful when the gate of Giant Despair's castle grated on its hinges at their flight.

For one second Fairfax stopped and listened; then hearing no sound save that made by the crickets and tree-toads without, he pushed the door boldly open, and rejoiced, like Hopeful, to find that it made less noise at the bold thrust than at the timid attempt. Across the green he crept, striving to keep as much as possible in the shadow of the house; for the moon made every object on which its light fell, clear as day. Past the out-buildings he strode, and groped his way through the gloom of the pine woods to the stable door. "What if the stable men were still on duty! What if the dogs were loose!" But no; all was silent, save that as he opened the door Peggy turned her head and whinnied low.

"Be quiet, Peggy!" he said softly, while he stroked the nose she laid against his shoulder as he rapidly slipped the bridle over her neck. "We will leave the saddle and all our Dutch trappings behind," said he, "and I will try if I have forgot the trick of bareback riding."

Feeling once more in his bosom to make sure of the paper, he threw off his coat and stepped noiselessly across the turf, and, leading Peggy by the bridle, passed down the dark path and out at the gate. Once fairly on the open road, he stopped, and leaping on Peggy's back he cried, "Now for it! 'tis a ride for life, and for that which is worth more than both our lives, my girl!"

On they sped, past field and forest. Ever and anon Fairfax paused, more than half expecting to hear galloping hoofs and dogs in full cry; but save for a startled deer trampling the underbrush in haste to get away, no sound broke on his ear. Boynton still slept his drunken sleep, and the hands of the old Dutch clock still marked the half-hour after eleven.

"A fig for the Boynton motto!" cried Fairfax, as he drew rein at last by the little strip of beach whence he had set out less than twenty-four hours ago. "I seem to have escaped its curse unscathed."

The moon had set, and the darkness was so great that save for the whiteness of the sand Fairfax would have been in some doubt whether he had found the meeting-place; but as he whistled thrice the familiar skiff put out from under the cypress trees, and Fairfax leaped aboard, holding Peggy by the bridle. In the darkness he could discern nothing more than the figure of the boatman muffled to the eyes in his great cloak. He nodded but spoke not as Fairfax sank into the stern, too weary for greeting; but his mind was full of satisfaction. Fortune had favored him throughout. Despite the rashness of his visit to Rosemary, he could not regret it, — for had it not brought him assurance beyond his wildest hopes of Penelope's favor? Even this, he felt, would have been too dearly bought had it hampered in the least his mission; but no, that was done, accomplished with brilliant success. Now there was naught before him but to rest his tired body and rejoice in the thought of Bacon's joy. This suggestion of his chief's delight brought new vigor, and sitting up for the first time Fairfax saw that the stream was more than half crossed, but saw also with surprise that the boatman had drawn in his oars. As Fairfax lifted his eyes they looked straight into the barrel of a pistol held level with his face. *Treachery!* — it took him but a fraction of a second to see that, and less than the same time to decide upon his own course. What man this was before him, who had betrayed him, or what had been the motive, he had no time to conjecture, — death stared him in the face.

Luckily for Fairfax, he had a swiftness of perception which waited not on the slow workings of reason. Instinct told him that one thing only could save him, and that one thing he did like a flash of lightning, — *he capsized the skiff!*

As the boat turned, the boatman, after floundering for some moments, caught the gunwale, and clambering upon the keel bestrode it in safety, while the brisk breeze blew him steadily down stream. Waiting not to inquire into his fate, Fairfax kicked off the Dutchman's big boots, struck out lustily for the Gloucester bank, and Peggy followed loyally. The water was cold, and Fairfax, wearied as he was by the day's work, had scarce force to resist its benumbing chill. As he felt his limbs stiffening and his faculties growing drowsy, his mind dwelt strangely on the motto over the fireplace at the Boynton plantation, — "Death to him who harms me!" He was not free from the superstition of his age, but he set his teeth in stern resolve to disprove the omen. He could not, he *would* not, die till he had placed the paper in Bacon's hands; then let the curse fall when it would.

Yet the last two rods proved almost too much even for his iron will; and when he felt land beneath him he could scarce gather strength to wade ashore, but was like to have drowned in three feet of water. His horse was well-nigh as exhausted as himself, — together they sank on the pebbly strand, quite vanquished by fatigue; but Fairfax felt in his soul a mighty joy and thankfulness, which rose superior to all bodily weakness, which overmastered all anger, all curiosity as to the how and why of the boatman's treachery — all this could wait; nothing mattered much, for — *he had the King's Commission.*

CHAPTER VIII.

LAODICEANS.

"I would that ye were either hot or cold."

IT was after sunrise before Fairfax had recovered from his exhaustion enough to push on. Rising at length from his hard bed, he limped along painfully, holding Peggy by the bridle. On his way he passed the hut of the boatman. As he had anticipated, it was empty. The owner had fled. "Gone to join Berkeley I'd be sworn," muttered Fairfax. "Well, I wish His Excellency joy of the addition to his forces. Could we send him all the other traitors in our camp it would be more gain to our cause than the winning of a pitched battle."

A little farther on Fairfax came upon the house of a farmer, who gladly gave him breakfast, together with grain and watering and a soft bed on the hay for Peggy. Richly did man and horse enjoy their well-earned rest; but when the sun-dial before the farmer's house marked eleven, Fairfax's eagerness and impatience got the better of bodily fatigue, and he resolved to attempt the five-mile journey which lay between him and Gloucester Court House, where Bacon's camp lay. Short as the distance was, it was yet no trifle for a man whose horse was jaded with travel and whose limbs were aching in every joint from cold and weariness. So slowly did they journey that noon was long overpast when they reached the camp. A very different figure was this dusty, way-worn, bedraggled traveller from the gallant, bravely clad soldier who had set out thence less than two days since.

The sentry looked and wondered at him as he passed, scarcely recognizing him; but he would not in any case have stopped him, for General Bacon had this day summoned all the men of Gloucester County to meet him at the Court House, to take the oath of allegiance to himself and swear to oppose the forces of Sir William Berkeley, as well as any troops coming out of England, until they should have opportunity to learn the King's will. This last clause in the oath which Bacon would have them take troubled the Gloucester men; for read it as they might, and with whatever juggle of plausible interpretation subtle Mr. Lawrence might put upon it, the matter smacked too much of treason for their taste. Yet with Bacon's army in the midst of them and Berkeley's army far away across the bay at Accomac, and with the Governor's threat to make the rivers of Virginia run with their blood because they would not rally round his standard last July, these poor hesitating Gloucester men found themselves between the devil and the deep sea, and wished petulantly that Bacon and Berkeley would fight it out betwixt them without dragging into the controversy peaceable planters who asked only to remain neutral.

Yet they had gathered this day, six hundred strong, to hear what Bacon had to say in the matter. Poor fools, who thought to escape from the magnetism of that form and face and voice and all-compelling personality with any will or judgment of their own!

The throng had the air of those whistling to keep their courage up, and verily none could disguise the fact that this day's business was of serious moment. Each man discoursed vehemently to his neighbor, for all that neighbor was talking as loudly as himself.

"I knew some ill would befall since ever those ominous presages did appear,—three in one year," quoth one.

"Yea," added another, "dost thou not bear in

mind that great comet, streaming like a horse's tail to westward?"

"That do I, and the flight of pigeons stretching their length over half the heavens, till they seemed past all numbering, and how when they lighted their weight broke down the limbs of the trees."

"Ay," said a third, "and worst of all, those swarms of flies last spring, that were no bigger than the top of my hand's littlest finger, yet did they come in such numbers that they devoured every young sprout, till the country was like a man shorn of his eyelids under the blazing sun of summer."

"Well, well!" broke in Fairfax, who had caught the words as he stood behind the yeoman. "Of what avail is all this talk of signs and portents? What is writ is writ, — and for the matter o' that your omens may be twisted either way. For mine own part, I do read in the swarms of flies the petty exactions and tyrannies of Governor Berkeley; in the wild pigeons, the Indians put to flight by our men; and in the streaming comet, the glorious career of General Bacon."

"Faith, ye speak truth: 'tis strange we ne'er thought on that interpretation," said all three in a breath, their mouths agape; yet one ventured: "'T is clear the omens do be in our favor and the chances promise fair, unless the King take offence; but there, to my mind, the hitch lies. Should His Majesty see fit to send soldiers over from home, what then? Methinks we should all walk wet-shod in blood, as the Governor threatened a while ago."

"Pish! Pish!" quoth another, with ill concealed contempt. "As to that, good master, we are in over shoes now, and might as well be in over boots. Besides, we must needs make answer for our conduct to Bacon as well as to Berkeley."

But a timid man with the white feather in his hat, which did but fitly shadow forth the white feather in his heart, stammered forth, while his knees shook under him, "Yes — but — but what about the English soldiers?"

At this a woman (for women as well as men were mingling in the throng in the field at Gloucester Court House that day), — a woman, I say, picked up a stick which lay in the trodden grass, and, breaking it across her knee, she waved the pieces above her head, shouting aloud so that all could hear her: "I for one fear the power of England no more than this broken stick."

"Ah!" cried Fairfax, approvingly. "'T is bravely spoke, and should go far to teach their duty to those who stand cowering around you calling themselves men, yet waiting for a woman to lead them." Under his breath he said: "By Heavens! 'tis the wife of Drummond; it is well none have recognized her." Then aloud: "But let us not waste time bandying words here, for the General himself is speaking from yonder hillock; and his words shall soon persuade you to his following, I will warrant you."

So saying Fairfax moved toward the little knoll in the centre of the camp. His heart leaped up to see his Chief standing there with the whole multitude gazing up at him and hanging upon his accents as he spoke. Too little has been made of the individuality of the voice; for nothing more betrays the character behind it, and nothing more surely affects the listener before it. Some voices are like a file, that rasps the nerves of the hearer. Some are like a brook, whose murmuring lulls to drowsy acquiescence. This man's was like an organ; and as one stop or another was touched, it could utter soft persuasion, or kindle to action, or strike with terror, or lead on to victory, and if need be to death.

The first words which caught the ear of Fairfax as he joined the throng at the foot of the natural platform whereon Bacon stood were words of pleading and calm argument.

"We the commons of Virginia do desire a prime union among ourselves against the common enemy. Let not the faults of the guilty be the reproach of the innocent, the crimes of your oppressors divide and separate those who have suffered by their oppression. The question is now before you. Men of Gloucester, will ye take the oath and join our ranks, or must we count you of the number of the foes of liberty?"

Silence — dead, leaden silence — followed this appeal; then from the midst of the crowd who had huddled close together as if to avoid individual recognition, a sandy-haired man spoke out timidly: "May it please you, Master Bacon, we have talked over this matter in conclave before our coming hither, and it is the sense of us Gloucester men that we are resolved to lend aid neither to you nor yet to Berkeley. As we told the Governor three months since, we do prefer to remain neutral."

"Neutral!" echoed Bacon, with a taunting mockery. "Oh, yes, ye are of those who would fain be saved with the righteous and yet do naught toward obtaining of the salvation. Zounds! I swear ye shall *not* remain neutral. He that is not for us is against us."

The General's fiery ardor began to burn into the coldness of the crowd; but still they strove to temporize and delay, if they could not evade, the final decision. The commoner men of the throng were with Bacon. For all they had walked many miles to the meeting and were spent with weariness, their spirits leaped within them at the cry of this champion of popular liberty. Instinctively they felt that his cause was theirs, and as instinctively Bacon, looking into their eyes, felt their response; but the men on horseback, the rich planters, the aristocracy already sprung up in this new democratic country, still stood cold and impassive as a stone.

At length one, Colonel Gouge, an officious busybody always anxious to make himself noticed, called aloud: "Perchance, Master Bacon, the oath may yet be taken if you grant us time. Thus far ye have chiefly spoke to the foot and not to the horse."

"Nay," cried Bacon, hotly; "I spake to the *men*, and I leave you to speak to the *horse*, as one beast can best understand another."

A ripple of resentment ran through the crowd. "Have a care, Mr. Bacon," cried a man dressed in the garb of a Church of England clergyman; "we are not come hither to hear our spokesman insulted."

"Faith," answered Bacon, now quite beside himself with passion, "if ye are not come to hear it, ye may stay to hear it. As for you, reverend sir, I would have you know it is your place to preach in church but not in camp. In the pulpit you may say what you please, but here you shall say what pleaseth me,—unless indeed ye can fight to better purpose than ye preach. 'T is not for a parson to teach a general the rules of war."

"If you be in sooth a general," called out a surly cavalier, "show us your commission. I know you but as a rebel whom the Governor hath outlawed, and cancelled the commission which you did wring from him by force and duress yonder at James City. Show your commission and we will follow you!"

"Will you so?" cried a voice from the thickest of the crowd. "Then stand by your words, for General Bacon's commission is *here!*"

A mighty cheer greeted Fairfax's words, though as yet the crowd scarce comprehended their purport.

When Bacon's eye fell upon the paper as Fairfax waved it above his head, he stopped short in the speech he was about to utter, staggered, and, catching at his heart, said to Drummond, who stood next him: "I am faint. Lend me thine arm to my tent."

Lawrence, who stood by, took in the situation at a glance, and while Drummond led Bacon away he took his place, and cried so that all could hear: "See! Your failure to stand by him like men hath cut him to the quick. This faintness which hath come upon him is but the result of all he hath endured in the behalf of your poor languishing country, which lies gasping under the violent pressure of unreasonable men. An ye make not common cause with him, I do promise you ye shall all suffer the like tyranny which hath worn him out. Ye shall see as he did, your servants slain and your plantations laid waste, the corn ye have sown reaped by the hands of savages red with the blood of the planter. All this, ay, and more, would come to pass should Berkeley chance to win in this strife wherein we do now be engaged. But win he will not, win he cannot; for this is a struggle betwixt a youth in the full vigor of his manhood and a graybeard in his dotage, betwixt an honest man and an old treacherous villain. Now Bacon hath his commission, naught can stay his triumph."

Here the orator paused; and then with a solemnity which struck awe to the hearts of those who heard, he said slowly: "Choose ye this day whom ye will serve."

The words of Lawrence made a deep impression.

Man turned to man and repeated them in awe-struck whispers. Under cover of the buzz Lawrence turned to Fairfax, exclaiming below his breath: "For God's sake go to the General! I like not his look."

Fairfax, who had been but biding his time lest he rouse suspicion of something amiss by haste, waited no urging, but quickly working his way to the outer circle of the crowd, was off like arrow from the bow. At the tent he met Drummond coming out.

"How is he?" asked Fairfax, breathlessly.

"Better," answered Drummond. "Belike 't was but the weakness of a moment; yet I own the General hath seemed to me a sick man since we came to this Gloucester shore. His head is over-hot, and his eye brighter than nature kindled it, and for his temper,—'t is perpetually at fever heat, and leapeth to his tongue on the slightest provocation."

"Stand not there prating like idiots," cried a voice from within the tent. "Either come in or move on."

Drummond shrugged his shoulders and passed on, glancing expressively at Fairfax, who hesitated an instant, then lifted the flap and entered. He was shocked at the ravages of disease, which his brief absence enabled him to perceive the more clearly.

"General," he exclaimed, "I am sore bestead to see thee thus."

"To see me how?" asked Bacon, testily, forgetting, or choosing to ignore, his confessions at Green Spring. But Fairfax answered steadily, "To see thee feverish in body and mind."

"What mean you by feverishness of mind?"

"I mean the temper which led you to speak so hotly to the crowd but now."

"Major Fairfax, I will be the judge of mine own words and mine own condition."

Fairfax was cut by this use of his title, which seemed to say that this conversation was held not as friends, but as officers, and that advice to a superior was strangely out of place. He bowed with a ceremony curiously ill matching with his draggled and dishevelled attire. "I stand reproved," he said, "and can but beg General Bacon's permission to retire."

Bacon's answer was made by rising from the stool on which he sat and flinging his arm over his companion's shoulder.

"Fairfax," he said low and sadly, "'t is God's truth you speak. I am ill, — ill in body and soul. Grant me but one more week to struggle with

Berkeley and I will have my foot on his neck — and then — why, then you and the rest must follow up the victory, for I am a spent ball."

"Say not so I pray thee," cried Fairfax, "for there be those do love thee more than life."

"Ay, lad, I do well believe it, of thee at least; but for a true man there is much beside his own life to live for. Could we but see this Virginia of ours with limbs unshackled, standing free and powerful, a Virgin Queen of the West, ruling in her own right, — there were a work well worth the cost of a thousand lives like thine and mine, — ay, Bryan?"

Never before had Fairfax heard his first name uttered thus familiarly by his Chief. It touched him inexpressibly; for it was as if they stood already in the white light of eternity, where all formalities and all petty distinctions of age and rank drop away and leave us all man to man. He could find no words to answer, but only grasped the hand which lay over his shoulder. After a minute, which seemed to have transformed him from a youth to a man, he answered with a deep gravity: "For my own poor life, my Chief, I dedicate it wholly to you, — to you and Virginia; but realizing as I do how the welfare of the province is bound up with yours, I must make bold, even at the risk of incurring anew your displeasure, to pray you have a care. To-day you are easily the first man in Virginia, and can mould events to your will. Let but a rumor go abroad that your health is unsound, and all is lost. Of what avail your commission an ye can not bear it?"

"Ah! the commission," cried Bacon, with a start. "My sickness had nigh drove it from my head. Tell me how ye did secure it. You be such a modest fellow, and make so little of exploits which others would proclaim with a trumpet, that ye are likely to be balked of your deserts; but of a surety this deed has earned rich reward."

"Dear Chief, if in very truth you think my deed entitled to reward, let me receive it in the acceptance of my counsel. Listen; I would have thee ride with me this night to Major Pate's house, where thou canst have nursing such as this rude camp can never offer. I will attend thee, and we will banish all the family and servants, that none may prate of thy condition."

A mighty cheering broke in on the last words of Fairfax, and at the same moment Drummond burst in, crying: "They have signed, General. They have taken the oath, every one!"

"So?" exclaimed Bacon. "Methinks the business hath moved too fast. Easy take, easy break. Still, with no resistance to be looked for in this direction I am as good as master of Virginia, if only — nay, no more weakness — Fairfax dear lad, order horses when thou wilt, so it be after thou art rested and day has broken. The morrow morn, Drummond, I go for a brief rest to Pate's Plantation. Upon you and Lawrence will devolve the charge of the army. Let no jealousies nor strife for precedence between you stir up dissensions in the troops. If you would make head against Berkeley, you must be unanimous amongst yourselves. Fairfax, give me my commission. Now leave me both, and I will set mine affairs in order and be ready to ride ere daybreak. The less said of mine absence, the better. Good night, gentlemen."

As Bacon stalked out, a negro stood at the door of the tent, bearing a covered basket in one hand, and in the other a pair of squawking hens much discomfited to find themselves dangling head downward before their time.

"Any poultry to-day, suh?" asked the black man.

Bacon was too much absorbed in his own thoughts to heed the presence of the man; but Drummond, who with Lawrence followed close after the General, answered somewhat gruffly: "Off with you!

We have neither time nor heart now to be planning for table dainties."

"Hold on there!" cried the voice of Fairfax from within the tent; "I have had little to eat to-day, and am spent with fasting. Come in, and I will strike a bargain with you. If ye will kill, dress, and cook your squawking hens within the half hour, ye shall have a shilling apiece for them."

The man grinned with a delight which closed his eyes and showed his glistening white teeth. Waiting no second bidding, he set down his basket and sat down cross-legged at the open flap of the tent. When Lawrence and Drummond had passed out of sight, however, he mysteriously drew the basket within the tent and let down the flap, as though he feared detection, though none were in sight. His precautions were not useless, however; for not long after a man in clothes lately cleansed and dried stole near to the tent and laid his ear close to the canvas.

"Ah," said Arthur Thorn to his base heart, "in time perhaps for one more state secret wherewith to make my peace with Berkeley. It was worth the risk I took. But could I only have got the commission and seen Fairfax at the bottom of the river —" His thoughts were interrupted by a few words which he caught from within the tent, — words of such portent that he resolved when the negro came out, to sift them, cost what it might. Fairfax had not recognized him in the boat,— of this he was sure, — and he resolved to make one more effort to work his revenge, and to strike at the honor where he had failed to reach the life. He went in and hailed as comrade the man at whose heart his pistol had been pointed. Truly Penelope Payne had given him no more than his due when she called Arthurn Thorn a Judas.

CHAPTER IX.

THE VALLEY OF THE SHADOW.

"Nothing can cover his high fame but Heaven,
No pyramids set off his memories
But the eternal substance of his greatness,
To which I leave him."

IT was night at Pate's Plantation. The rain beat against the window-pane.

A smouldering log laid across the iron fire-dogs dimly lighted up the interior of the low-raftered room, wherein, gathered about a table, sat three men. One who had seen them last in the splendor of that September morning at Green Spring would scarce have recognized the high-hearted, triumphant soldiers who then gathered around General Bacon, in these bowed, sorrow-stricken men.

Gloom, deep as the night without, sat upon their brows, and their voices echoed the dirge of the wind as it sighed and sobbed through the pines at the door. They spoke in low murmurs, and ever and anon cast glances at a shadowy corner where stood a rude bed, on which, sharply outlined beneath the canvas sheet, lay the form of a man, — still with that awful, rigid stillness which death alone lends. It was the corpse of Nathaniel Bacon. Yes, there he lay, — he who had hurled defiance at outnumbering foes, he who had led a forlorn hope and transformed it to a conquering army, he who had borne an unmoved and lofty courage through all perils and difficulties, now lay there like the dullest yokel who had fired a cannon at his bidding. Death, the leveller who wipes out all distinctions 'twixt bravery and cowardice, intellect and impotence, power and weakness, had passed over him and left him — thus.

"Who could credit," said Fairfax at length, speaking more to himself than to those about him, and uttering the words with effort, as though they encountered some obstacle in his throat, — "who could credit that 't is scarcely a month since he put Berkeley's whole army to rout and sent them flying across the bay to Accomac!"

"Yes," responded Drummond; "but four weeks since he did enter Jamestown with banners flying, with captives and trophies for all the world like a triumphal procession, and set the houses ablaze in a glorious bonfire to the victory of liberty — alas and alas! Now he lies yonder, and all he fought for lost in the loss of him."

"Nay," burst out Fairfax, "the cause of liberty is oft more forwarded by the martyr than by the victor, and none who struggle valiantly for the right shall have struggled in vain."

The young man's voice rose and fell with that instinctive unconscious rhythm which in moments of deep grief or passion makes all men poets.

Silence fell after his words, then Lawrence spoke. "Fairfax, you alone were with him when he died, — though we came on the wings of the wind at your summons, yet, alas, too late! How came the end?"

"Why, thus: For three days he lay there on the cot where you see him, first white as the sheet above him, then flushed, and tossing restlessly to and fro; and ever and anon when I did go to him to cover his limbs or moisten his parched mouth, I caught him murmuring of early life in the home country, of his courtship, and then of his coming hither to Virginia, and once he raved of poison; for, to say truth, he did have it heavily on his mind that he had met with foul play."

"What!" cried Lawrence, starting up from his chair as if the thought stung him beyond endurance, "could it have been?"

"I know not for sure," answered Fairfax. "'Tis hard to think any man with English blood in his veins could thus foully do to death the foe he could not conquer by fair means; but Berkeley's situation was waxing desperate."

"Yet poison!" broke in Lawrence, "*poison*— oh, I cannot think it! Besides, these Virginia marshes in the chill mornings and damp evenings of autumn do breathe out a miasma more deadly than any drug."

"Yea," said Fairfax, "I do myself be persuaded that 't is this hath laid him low,— this and the chafing of his too eager soul. Knowing that he was all in all to the cause, he did strain his weakened body to work too heavy for it. Oh would to God my mean life could have been accepted as a sacrifice for his!"

Of a sudden, as he spoke, he seemed to see the motto writ before his vision in the air, "*Pereat qui me lacessit.*" To his over-wrought mind it appeared that the curse was wreaking itself; that passing himself, as a tool too insignificant for vengeance, it had fallen on the head which had planned the deed, the head now laid low in unfeeling death. The grief of the honest young heart was too great to be borne. Laying his head upon his arms on the table, he sobbed aloud.

"Come, Fairfax," said Lawrence, kindly laying his hand upon the bowed shoulder, "these tears do but unfit us for the service we yet may render. God knows no man hath greater cause for sorrow than I. Grief for the dead is but rosemary and rue unless there be mingled therewith the bitter weed of remorse. This it is which doth rankle in my heart,— the thought that when he lived I knew him so little, and did in my vanity and self-esteem hold myself the mainstay of this our cause. Now, alas, I am learning how much I am to seek in that greatness which did ever mark him."

Ere Lawrence had finished speaking the sound of hurried footsteps was heard without, and with no knock to herald him a breathless youth thrust the door open and hurled himself into the room, followed by a gust of wind and rain. His leather leggings were scratched and torn by bush and brier, his coat hung in tatters, he had lost his hat, and his hair was in wild disorder. "Fly!" he panted. "Fly! I am come at the risk of my life to warn you — all is lost — Berkeley is returned from Accomac stronger than ever. The Gloucester men have forgot their oaths and set out to join him. He hath caught a rumor of Bacon's sickness, and vows he will have him alive or dead. He hath set a price upon his head, and swears he will have it set up above the gate at Middle Plantation."

"Saith he so indeed!" quoth Fairfax, rising with set lips and eyes glowing lantern-like beneath his brows. "Saith he so? Then let us set ourselves to thwart him once more, — yea, though our own lives do pay the forfeit, as indeed they are like enough to do in any case." The young man spoke with a vigor and intensity of purpose which dominated his companions. The mind which has a ready-developed scheme will always rule doubt and indecision.

"Give me your cloak, Drummond," continued Fairfax, "and you yours, Lawrence; but first give me Bacon's sword, and let us bind it upon him, — for sure none other will ever be found worthy to wear it after him, — and here — " Pausing an instant, he went to a high desk which stood in the corner of the room, and, pressing a spring, drew out a secret drawer, from which he took the white paper with the red seal, — the commission for which he had struggled so hard and dared so much, and all now as it seemed for naught. "*Pereat qui me lacessit,*" he murmured. "May it hold true now if never before. A curse on any who shall disturb this in its sacred resting-place!" So speaking he closed the desk, and, stepping to the bed, he opened Bacon's coat and laid it reverently upon his heart.

"Now, friends, let us wrap him well, for the

night wind is sharp, and who knoweth whether or no the dead may feel it? Thou, Hanford," he added, turning toward the latest comer, who had but just got his breath, "take the lantern and go before to the boat down yonder, which you will unmoor and have ready for our coming; for I do purpose that we commit this sacred body to the care of the stream he loved, trusting that the river will keep our secret so well that no man shall know his resting-place. For a time his name must bleed; but sure as there is a God in heaven, justice shall some day be done to his memory. Farewell, my Chief, my friend, my glory, and my hope; farewell!" Speaking thus, he bent over and kissed the pale cold forehead streaked with dark hair. Each man present followed his example. Then they lifted their solemn burden and filed out of the little room, leaving the door wide behind them and the dying embers blackening on the cold hearth.

The tempest shook them as they passed down the wet and slippery path which led to the shore, and the night lowered black around them; but by the fire-fly glimmer of Hanford's lantern they guided their footsteps to the beach. The wet trees dropped fresh tears upon them as they passed beneath the dripping boughs. Silently they laid their burden on the bottom of the boat, and with it two large stones of such weight that Fairfax sweated with the task of lifting them. Lawrence then took his place in the prow, looking forward like some stern, strange figure-head.

Drummond sat in the stern and Fairfax and Hanford took the oars. "Lawrence," said Fairfax, "it shall rest with you to decide where we shall pause."

"So be it," answered Lawrence; and then there was silence save for the dashing of the wind-swept waves against the little craft.

When they were come to a spot in the very centre of the stream, where the water was deepest and blackest, Lawrence said slowly: "We have come far enough. Here be his resting-place, and may he sleep well!"

Fairfax drew in his oar, and with the help of Drummond and Hanford wrapped the stones in the cloaks and bound them securely to the body. Tenderly as ever mother raised her dead babe they lifted the corpse over the side of the boat, held it a moment, then solemnly and slowly let it fall.

A plash, a widening circle of ripples, then all was as before. The little boat was turned about and headed for the shore. When it touched, the four men stepped out and stood silent, looking into each other's eyes with that sense of kinship born of a common deep experience. Then they struck hands, and vowed that, come what might, no man should learn the secret of that sacred burial. After that they parted, going every man his own way.

The great rebellion was ended. The bond which had held it together was snapped, the mainspring broken. Another month and the forces once so near to victory were scattered, the leaders a handful of hunted outlaws. Lawrence had fled for safety to the morasses of the great woods; Drummond and Fairfax lay prisoners in the hands of their arch-enemy; but Bacon had escaped, — death had hidden him safe from all the venom of those who sought to drag him down.

> "He's gone from hence unto a higher court
> To plead his cause, where he by this doth know
> Whether to Cæsar he was friend or foe."

CHAPTER X.

VENGEANCE.

*" Who will not mercie unto others show
How can he mercie ever hope to have? "*

BEFORE the Court House at Middle Plantation, on the green which now might more properly have been called the *brown*, so hard and sere was it beneath the frosts of the bitter December of 1676, stood a group of men and women awaiting the roll of the drum which should shortly sound forth a summons to all whom it might concern to attend the sitting of the Governor for the trial by martial law of the *White Aprons*, the companions in arms of that rebel and factious disturber of the peace, the late Nathaniel Bacon, whose rebellion had fallen to pieces like a pack of cards at his death.

"I tell you, neighbors, the Governor means to take order with these *White Aprons* after a fashion that shall never be forgot within the borders of the Old

Dominion." So spoke a man whose hard, stern face would have been at home among the grim-visaged dwellers by Massachusetts Bay. "Verily," he continued, "the scaffold is crying out for some of them."

"Ay," answered a younger man who stood by, rubbing his hands to keep them warm, "belike they have deserved all that can befall them; but the punishing of rebels is like the rolling of a wheel down hill, — the start is easy, but the trouble lies in stopping. One of these men is as guilty as another; and if the Governor hangs the first, he cannot in reason stay his hand till half the colony be strung up by the neck."

"Why not forgive them all?"

At these words, uttered in a high, childish treble, many turned their eyes toward the little maiden who stood holding tight to her father's hand, her hood outlining the full moon of her chubby face, and her long skirt bobbing against the ground.

"Tush, tush, child!" answered her father, vexed to have the attention of the crowd thus drawn upon him, and fearing perhaps lest the words of the child be held but the mirror of the parent's thought. "Leave forgiveness to those who deal with childish pranks like thine. Men must count the cost before they plot treason against the King and the State. 'To the scaffold with one and all!' say I."

"Nay; the child is nearer right than thou, my good master, else hath our religion gone sadly astray in its teachings."

The new voice which uttered these words spoke with evident authority; and as it was recognized, all the indented servants and freemen, and even the landed gentry, uncovered their heads in token of respect to Colonel Payne. Over his arm he held the bridle of his horse, while at a little distance a gray-haired negro was helping his daughter to alight. As soon as her foot touched the ground she too joined the throng just in time to catch her father's words. Straight as she stood, and bravely as she faced the crowd, the pallor of her cheek and the dark lines beneath her eyes told of some inner conflict.

"Ask them, father," said she, pressing closer to Colonel Payne's side, "whether they say not their prayers o' Sunday."

"Why, surely, Mistress Payne," said a woman's voice at her other side. "Methinks we were but half Christians did we not say them each night."

"Then," answered Penelope Payne, scornfully, "I do commend you to pray less and practise more; for an God forgave your trespasses as you forgive those that trespass against you, I pity your soul."

The men about tittered. Colonel Payne turned to his daughter with unwonted sternness on his brow and in his voice. "Stand not here, girl, bandying words for the amusement of the crowd," he said. "Get thee in to the Court House and I will shortly follow."

Even as he spoke the rumble of the drum sounded forth its rude summons, which brought all the stragglers trooping into the court-room, where with bare heads they awaited the coming of the Governor and his officers. When these had come in and taken their seats, making a brave show in that bare room with their rich dress, the common folk also sat down on the benches and awaited eagerly, as those at a play, the beginning of the life-and-death drama now about to be acted before them.

But there were those in that assembly to whom this morning's business meant an hour of suspense, a day of agony, and a life-time of sadness, — those who were destined to behold husband and father and son snatched from their arms and hurried away to ignominious death.

When all were settled a corporal appeared, leading Arthur Thorn. His face wore a look of humility and penitence, full of disgusting hypocrisy to those who knew him, and about his neck was a rope which some of those present devoutly wished were for use rather than ornament. Making his way forward to the bar before the Governor's chair, he flung himself upon his knees, and recited his confession and plea for pardon glibly enough, but in such a sing-song voice as showed clearly that he had learned it off by heart, parrot-like.

"I, Arthur Thorn," — so his confession ran, — "that all bystanders may take notice of this, my sincere repentance of my rebellion, do here most humbly, upon my knees, with a rope about my neck, implore pardon of God, my King, the Honorable Governor, Council, and magistrates of this His Majesty's country, and humbly crave the benefit of mercy and pardon."

Here he rolled his eyes heavenward, and uttered with assumed fervor the hollow prayer: "God save the King, and prosper the Governor and magistrates with all happiness and good success!"

"Hush!" — the word was passed around the crowd — "the Governor is rising to speak." There was leaning this way and that, and an eager craning of necks, as His Excellency began: —

"Arthur Thorn, for that you have been in arms against His Majesty and against me his vice-regent, you do richly deserve to forfeit your life after the manner symbolized by the rope about your neck; but whereas you did come out from among the enemy and have humbly sued for pardon, and whereas you have furnished us with valuable evidence against one of the prisoners soon to be brought before this tribunal, we do therefore in the King's name grant you pardon, and caution you never again to be associated with so heinous an offence."

Not a cheer was heard as the prisoner rose from his knees,—pardoned but despised. A vague fear shook the heart of Penelope as he passed her. She closed her eyes, unwilling to gaze upon him. When she looked up again he was gone, and in his place at the bar of judgment stood a red-haired, raw-boned man of little outward beauty, but with firmness, fortitude, and indomitable manhood writ large on his plain countenance.

"Prisoner, what is your name?"

"My name, may it please Your Excellency, and you, gentlemen of the Council, is Drummond, long known in Scotland, and later in this colony, as the name of an honest man."

"Mr. Drummond," answered the Governor with

a terrible politeness, "you are very welcome. I am more glad to see you than any man in Virginia. You shall be hanged in half an hour!"

"As Your Excellency pleases!" rejoined the prisoner, as calmly as though he had accepted an invitation to dine at Green Spring that same day.

Yet the crowd noted that he turned pale and trembled when he heard a groan behind him and recognized the voice of his wife. One of the commissioners leaned forward and whispered in the Governor's ear.

"So," said His Excellency, laying back his lips till the teeth seemed to stand out like those of a beast of prey ready to flesh themselves in the heart of the victim, "that groan I understand, comes from the same Sarah Drummond who not four months since did break a twig across her knee there in the field at Gloucester Court House and incite the Gloucester men to defy me by assuring them that she feared the power of England no more than that stick. Now, I dare be sworn she sings another tune."

At that the prisoner at the bar turned his back full on the Governor. "Sarah," cried he, "be firm! I charge you on these rings which we did exchange at our marriage that you forswear not yourself to renounce the cause of justice and liberty, fallen though it be!"

"Corporal, take off that ring with which he thus defies us, and let the prisoner be hanged before noon!" cried Berkeley in a fury.

It was easier said than done, for Drummond made so stout a resistance that four men could scarcely drag him from the room; nor could the ring be wrested from him till they had bound him, arms and legs, with ropes.

It was a disgraceful scene, and there were those in the crowd began to murmur, "Shame!" but it was under their breath, for none dared face the rage which had thus usurped the robes of justice.

"Call Cheeseman!" ordered the autocrat, and Major Cheeseman stood forth.

"What motive had ye to enter into this damnable treason and conspiracy?" asked Berkeley. Cheeseman opened his lips to speak; but ere he could utter a syllable, his young wife, all pale and trembling, rushed forward, and throwing herself at the Governor's feet, burst forth into an imploring petition, though her voice was choked with sobs. "My good Lord," she cried, scarce able to make herself heard, "I pray you give ear to my supplications. If any must be punished, sure 't is I should bear the burden, since 't was by means of my urgency and at my provocation that my husband did join his lot with that of Bacon. Therefore, an you would have your memory for bare justice go down to posterity without stain you must needs hang me and set my husband free."

"No, never! never! never!" cried her husband; but still she knelt there at the feet of the Governor. She might as well have knelt to a stone image, — nay, far better; for an image of stone could but have been deaf to her prayer, whereas this lofty gentleman answered her supplication with such insult as would pollute too far the pages of my story to set down. Thereafter he bade her hold her tongue, and with no more show of trial than had attended Drummond's sentence, Cheeseman too was dragged away to the guard-house.

Berkeley smiled; but it was a smile ill to look upon, — such a smile, doubtless, as sits on the face of Satan as he snatches one soul after another. Revenge but grows as it is fed, and never yet had any man enough to glut his appetite.

As the words of insult to the innocent and most unhappy young wife of Major Cheeseman fell upon the ears of the audience, there ran a universal shudder through the crowd, as though they feared the wild beast whom they had let loose. But one man there was who feared not to speak his mind, let the issue be what it might. As Colonel Payne saw Mistress Cheeseman sink to the earth, stricken down by the tyrant's words as by a dagger, his hand grasped the sword by his side as though he would draw it then and there in her defence; and as he saw her husband dragged from the court-room, he rose in his place, and, speaking calmly, though a spot of indignant red glowed on his cheek, he said:—

"May it please Your Excellency, and you, gentlemen of the Governor's staff, I ask ere another rebel be tried, as it were by court-martial, though in this building raised to the Civil Law, that your honorable body do consider whether the time is not come when it were safe to return to these unfortunate and fallen men the immemorial right of every free-born Englishman, — the right to a fair trial according to the law of the land."

Here the speaker was interrupted, both by cheers and hisses. None else but him had ever been allowed to proceed so far; but he went on still in that even tone of voice, while all around was so quiet that one could hear the rats scurrying about among the rafters while he paused.

"Have ye forgot," he continued, now half turning to those on the benches by his side, — "have ye forgot the provisions of your rich inheritance, the great charter, which sure hath suffered no sea change in its crossing of the ocean which lies betwixt us and home? 'No freeman,' says that instrument, 'shall be forejudged of life or limb, disherited, put to torture or death, neither shall he be disseized, out-lawed, exiled, or distroyed of his liberties, freeholds, and free customs, but by the lawful judgment of his peers. So that the judgment is by this fundamental law referred to the breasts and consciences of a jury.'"

At the word "jury," a mighty shout arose, so loud that it echoed in the rafters and lost itself in the open chambers of the eaves.

"A jury! a jury!" answered fifty voices at once.

"No more martial law!"

"Give the rebels their rights!"

As Berkeley listened to these tumultuous cries, his countenance grew ever blacker and sterner. Twice he turned to the sergeant to bid him enforce order; but the popular voice was too strong for him, and the popular will had made itself felt with a force not to be gainsaid.

Robert Beverley and Philip Ludwell, who sat side by side at the Governor's right hand, laid their heads together in earnest counsel, then drawing nearer they whispered thus in the ear of His Excellency:

"'T were best yield the point since the people have it so much at heart."

"Not I," rejoined His Excellency, fiercely. "Think ye I have fought with wolves to fear these whelps?"

"'T is but a semblance of yielding, whereby many a ruler hath conquered an unruly mob ere now," quoth Beverley.

"Besides," added Ludwell, "the Council be all of your way of thinking; so if thou dost declare a 'life and death' jury to be drawn from the body of loyal men it shall be as though thou thyself spake out of twelve mouths."

"There may be something in 't," admitted the Governor, reluctantly, but relaxing a trifle, and for the first time, the stern and fixed obstinacy of his determination.

"*Something* in it; there is *everything* in it," answered Ludwell, who had ever a great desire to stand well with the people, to conciliate while he ruled, and to hide the iron hand in the velvet glove. "But if thou wilt gain aught by the concession, grant it quickly, lest thou lose all by seeming to yield on sheer compulsion what now thou mayst grant as 't were of thy free will and exceeding goodness."

For an instant Berkeley listened, loath to risk his

autocracy, and yet more loath to lose his vengeance. Breathless the people awaited his decision, watching his face as though they read there the vacillations of his purpose.

At length his decision was taken, and rising to his feet he said: —

"People of Virginia, hearken now unto me. Though 't is certain that those subjects of His Majesty late in rebellion against him and me and all others in rightful authority are entitled to no show of mercy, and though to spare such were to encourage treason everywhere to show its ugly head without fear, lest it should be cut off, and though it was but for the good of the colony that martial law has so far been preserved, and though all know that I have been but the sword in the hands of the Council in the justice I have meted out, — yet for as much as ye do now cry out for civil trials for these wretches, confederates, and traitors to the people, I do yield my judgment in the matter, and declare for your satisfaction that hereafter all trials shall be by a life and death jury, drawn from among these loyal men and true who sit around me."

Scarcely had the Governor finished when such a wild scene shook the house as Middle Plantation had ne'er before witnessed at any assembly

Vengeance.

whatsoever of its people. There was throwing up of hats and hurrahs for Sir William Berkeley, the protector of Virginia liberties, and finally a rushing forth of the crowd as though their rejoicing was swollen to a greatness not to be contained within any four walls.

But the end was not yet.

CHAPTER XI.

THE TRIAL OF BRYAN FAIRFAX.

> "If I have freedom in my love
> And in my soul am free,
> Angels alone, that soar above,
> Enjoy such liberty."

IT was a morning in the beginning of January, 1676-7. His Excellency, the Governor of Virginia, with three associate judges drawn from the sixteen members of the Colonial Council, sat that day in a court of life and death at Middle Plantation, with a panel of jurors summoned from his loyal adherents.

If the haughty spirit of the vice-regent chafed at the restraint of their presence, his pride bowed not to even a semblance of humility. He bore himself with every whit as swelling a port as when in the previous month he administered drum-head justice (or injustice) to the unlucky wights dragged protesting before his court-martial. His temper had not grown more judicial in the interval of weeks.

Indeed it seemed as if time but deepened his sense of injury and made his hatred more intense. In short, Sir William Berkeley was Sir William Berkeley still. His mouth was hard and cruel; his eye was the eye of a tyrant,—shifty, suspicious, and overbearing; his nose was the nose of a bigot, —with pinched nostrils, which seemed to dilate but half way, and grudgingly, to the fresh air of heaven. Reader, when you meet with such a countenance, waste no time in argument or appeals. It were as idle to strive to reach the sympathy of the wild beast by tears, or to melt the heart of the rock with eloquence.

One who knew him well and saw him daily at this time wrote home: "Age and misfortune have withered his desires but not his hopes," whereby I take it he meant that all the hopes of this bitter old man were now centred in the destruction of the desires of others.

The same good folks who had watched the proceedings of the court-martial thronged the court again this morning, satisfaction swelling at their hearts and written on their faces as they turned them toward the twelve men who were seated in the jury-box,—a rough pen set off at one side of the court.

It troubled them very little to note that all the

faces in that jury belonged to stout King's men, strong in the traditions of the divine rights of sovereigns and their vice-regents, — men who were as like as Berkeley himself to mete out the branding iron and the gibbet to the men brought before them for the final sentence of "guilty" or "not guilty." But these colonists who crowd the court to-day are not of a squeamish constitution, and are in sooth by no means loath to look upon a fellow creature swinging high in air with rigid limbs and distorted, livid features, nor yet to behold bleeding quarters nailed to the stout iron-bound gates of the plantation; but they are Englishmen, — ay, English to the core, — and they demand that the victim be tried and convicted by due process of English law, not hurried away like cattle to the shambles at the will of a tyrant.

The English law of that time we must, however, bear in mind was as far removed from the law of our day as the taste of that age from ours. The colonies did but reflect the judicial customs of the mother country and her courts, wherein every judge, from Scroggs and Jeffreys down, badgered prisoners and browbeat witnesses and cowed juries into servile submission, while the suspected man was treated as a criminal, and forced to prove his innocence, if he could, with all odds against him.

The Trial of Bryan Fairfax.

The accused was denied the privilege of counsel except to advise him on questions of law, and could not be sworn as a witness in his own defence, though allowed to make statements, not under oath, to the jury.

It was a hard and unfeeling crowd which gathered on the benches that third day of January, 1677, to hear Bryan Fairfax tried for rebellion and treason, and condemned, as none present doubted he would be, to die on the gallows. One pale and delicate face alone quivered with intensity of feeling; but none saw it, for it was sheltered behind the veil which completely shrouded the features. But the very veil shook, as the clerk, all preliminaries ended, called the case of "The King against Bryan Fairfax."

As the summons ended, the prisoner walked down the room and stood up before the bar, his guard on either side bearing the axe, after the English fashion, with its blade turned away as if (oh, terrible irony!) in token of the unwillingness of the court to shed innocent blood.

Henry Hartwell, the clerk of the court, bade the sergeant-at-arms make proclamation.

"Oyez! Oyez! Oyez!" cried the sergeant, so rapidly that the crowd could scarcely hear the words as he jerked them out. "Sir William

Berkeley, Governor of Virginia, and Chief Justice of this court, chargeth and commandeth all manner of persons here assembled to keep silence and to sit with uncovered heads upon pain of imprisonment."

When those who sat below had uncovered their heads in due obedience, the sergeant turned and addressed the prisoner at the bar:

"Bryan Fairfax, hold up thy hand."

At these words all eyes were fixed on the prisoner. There he stood in the felon's dock, his face pallid, his eyes sunken; yet to one at least of those gathered in the court-room he looked the noblest and the goodliest man beneath the raftered roof that day.

"Bryan Fairfax," quoth the clerk, standing up as the sergeant-at-arms sat down, "thou dost stand indicted as a false traitor to the illustrious, serene, and most excellent prince, Charles Second, by the grace of God, of England, Scotland, France, Ireland, and Virginia, King and defender of the faith. The indictment whereon thou art now to be tried hath four several counts. First, that thou didst in July last incite the crowd gathered in the old field on the shores of the York River to open rebellion and to espousing the cause of one Nathaniel Bacon, he being in arms, and wickedly waging war against his lawful sovereign, the King."

The Trial of Bryan Fairfax.

"So ye found it out, did ye?" said the prisoner under his breath.

"Second, that thou didst thyself rise in arms against the King, and therefore art guilty of rebellion and treason."

"Third, that thou didst aid and abet the said Nathaniel Bacon in his treason and rebellion against the King in that thou didst steal and feloniously convey state papers to him from the house of Colonel Boynton; and, fourth and lastly, thou standest charged with the more particular offence of having attempted the life of His Majesty's vicegerent, Sir William Berkeley, the Governor of this said province of Virginia."

At these last words a tremor of excitement ran through the crowd.

"How says he?"

"Attempting the life of the Governor!"

"Why, that were naked murder."

"Bah! they will lose all by striving for too much; none will believe Fairfax an assassin."

"Silence in the court-room on pain of imprisonment!" cried the clerk; and as the hush fell he continued, turning once more to the prisoner at the bar: "How sayst thou, Bryan Fairfax; art thou guilty or not guilty?"

"Not guilty."

"Wilt thou submit to the judgment of this court, or wilt thou stand thy trial?"

"I will stand my trial."

"How wilt thou be tried?"

"By God and my country."

"God send thee a good deliverance!"

"Amen!" called a voice from the crowd. All turned to discover whence it came, but the confusion covered the speaker, and the trial went forward.

"Bryan Fairfax," the clerk continued, "listen to the names of those men whom thou shalt hear called to pass upon trial for thy life or death. If thou wilt challenge any, thou must challenge them when they come to the book to be sworn, before they be sworn. They are, as thou seest, all freeholders and housekeepers, as the law doth command. Here," he added, holding up the scroll so that Fairfax could see, "thou mayst read the list for thyself."

"I protest," said Fairfax, turning to Berkeley when he had by bending forward contrived to decipher the list of jurymen, "I do perceive in these men a forejudged sentence against me, for all of them be of the opposition."

"Opposed to traitors, ay," answered the Governor, sternly.

"Surely, Your Excellency will not have me thus assailed from the jury-box itself before my case is heard?"

"Faith," answered Berkeley, sneeringly, "methinks we have a full-fledged lawyer among us. Prithee, young man, where did ye study law to have your mouth so crammed with argument?"

"I did study law at the Temple Inns for two years ere ever I came to this poor country," Fairfax made calm response; "but sure it needs no schooling in subtleties of law to plead against a trial by one's enemies as opposed to fairness and common justice."

"These gentlemen are thine enemies but in that they are king's men, and since thy fellow rebels be still under the ban, thou canst scarce look to have a jury of thy peers."

The very word *rebels* seemed to excite Berkeley, for his face reddened, and his features worked as he proceeded.

"'T is idle to say more," said Fairfax, with a certain scorn in his tone, which cut, though it came from a man in bonds; "I ask that the clerk record my protest."

Scarcely waiting for his words to be finished, the Governor turned to the clerk and bade him swear the jury. Hartwell rose and summoned the jury to be sworn, saying to each and every man as he came forward to the open Bible:

"Lay your hand upon the book and look upon the prisoner. You shall well and truly try, and true deliverance make between our Sovereign Lord the King and the prisoner at the bar, whom you shall have in charge according to your evidence, so help you God."

When each man had thus sworn, the crier took his place and proclaimed: "Twelve good men and true, stand together and hear your evidence!"

Penelope Payne looked on these men, and for her life, knowing what she knew of them, could think of nothing but the jury tried to call Faithful, in a story she had lately read called the "Pilgrim's Progress," by one Bunyan (himself a prisoner), and writ, so they said, in jail.

When these gentlemen were sat down, the crier once more made proclamation: "Oyez! if any one can inform the King's justices in regard to the crimes charged against the prisoner, let him come forth and he shall be heard; for now the prisoner stands at the bar upon his deliverance. The attorney for the Crown will now set forth the indictment."

Jauntily, as though he had set himself to ease the man before him of a purse or a game-bag instead of his life, the public prosecutor rose and began his speech; but as he went on he succeeded in lashing himself into a fury of eloquence which could deceive none, for all heard the state coin jingling behind the thunder of his voice: —

"Gentlemen of the jury," quoth he, in tones of professional solemnity, "you have heard the indictment read. You have heard the substance thereof opened. It is short in words, but high in consequence — *treason!* 'T is a mighty crime, and one which no man can commit and live when detected and apprehended."

"Oh," cried Penelope Payne softly to her own heart, nearly broken with anguish, "that any man should seek the life of another in cold blood, — 't is past believing."

The prosecutor continued: "Lese-Majesty would set at naught all traditions, all sanctions, all sanctities, and tread under foot all that makes life dear and honorable. All this the prisoner at the bar hath done, as we will show you by many witnesses, who will proclaim him out of his own mouth a traitor and a rebel; and as though this general crime wherein he is knit and bound together with those who have already paid for their fault with their lives and whose blood cries aloud to him to join them on the scaffold, were not enough, this person hath descended to the deeper and more particular iniquity of the assassin."

"'T is false!"

The deep voice of Fairfax rang out like hammer on anvil, crashing down upon the smooth glibness of the public prosecutor.

"Ay, is it so?" the prosecutor made response in a tone of insolent irony. "We have your word for it, — the word of a rebel and a traitor!"

The hand of Fairfax fumbled as though feeling for his sword; then realizing his helplessness he cast but one glance of indignation at his tormentor, and then addressing the Bench he continued in calmness:

"The accusation of attempting the life of the Governor I have repelled with the scorn befitting an officer and a gentleman. Poison is the weapon of a coward and a miscreant. No follower of Bacon hath ever employed it against a foe."

At this there went a murmur about the court; for 't was openly circulated that General Bacon had been foully taken off after that fashion. The justices writhed on the bench, and Berkeley grew red as fire, and muttered under his breath: "Faith, the rope shall choke that insolent tongue of his!"

Penelope Payne, watching the jury, saw all brows darken, and her heart sank within her.

The Trial of Bryan Fairfax.

"We care not for your asserting unless ye have proof," cried the Governor. "We will hear your witnesses, but not you till ye have a chance to cry for pardon."

"So," says Fairfax, coolly, "you have already decided on my conviction. Your Honors, I do protest against being tried thus before the man I am accused of striving to murder. Is it not written in the statutes of England that no man shall sit in judgment on a case wherein himself is interested? How much more when that interest extendeth to his life! 'T is not possible that I be fairly heard on the final count of my indictment while Sir William Berkeley sitteth in that chair."

At this there went a mighty buzzing about the room. The jurors leaned together, and the justices announced that they would retire for the consideration of that matter.

Within the court-room opinion wavered now this way, now that: "His point is ill taken."

"Nay, he hath right on his side."

"The Governor will never yield,— yet let him not try the temper of the people too far."

"He is in a fury."

"Well, he 'd best beware lest his fire burn his own hand in the end."

"Hush, they are coming back!"

Such silence fell that all could hear the footsteps of the judges in the passage-way, and all marked their faces as they entered.

"We have considered the question raised by the prisoner," quoth Ludwell, "and we are of one mind in the matter. Feeling that the life of the Governor is one with the life of the State, and since he hath been appointed of the King to sit in all trials for rebellion and treason, he is of law qualified to sit in this. The prosecutor may go on."

Fairfax again bade the clerk record his protest, and then continued: —

"For the first count I do acknowledge that I bade the Gloucester men stand firm for Bacon, but I did not incite them to bear arms against the King, but *for* him." The clerk busily took down his words, whilst the few friends of the prisoner in the crowd shook their heads, grieved to see him thus putting the noose around his own neck.

"Then," quoth the prosecutor, "we will not waste the time of the court in proving what is confessed, for Nathaniel Bacon and all those aiding and abetting him were long since duly proclaimed and adjudged rebels against their King, and the accused admits inciting others to the same treason. We will pass to the second count, wherein thou standest charged with having been in arms against the king."

The Trial of Bryan Fairfax.

The prosecutor smiled a bland, oily smile, as one who sees his game dropping into his hands without the trouble of firing a shot. "Bryan Fairfax, we are prepared to prove by many witnesses that thou wert seen foremost in the van of the rebel army at the Green Spring trench and among the burning houses of Jamestown. Dost thou acknowledge this also?"

"I acknowledge bearing arms with Bacon at Green Springs, but not as a rebel against the King," answered Fairfax; and again the prosecutor smiled. "No doubt," said he, "thou wilt as readily assent to the third count of the indictment, wherein thou standest charged with the stealing and feloniously conveying to Bacon from the house of Colonel Boynton, where it had been lodged for safe keeping, a state paper of grave importance. How sayst thou as to this?"

"I desire to know what state paper I am charged with taking," said Fairfax, quietly.

"Call Benjamin Boynton!"

Ere his name was uttered, the giant form of Big Boynton was seen elbowing its way through the crowd to the witness-stand.

"Look upon the prisoner! Hast seen him ere now?"

At the question the giant slowly opened his red

eyes, which he ordinarily held half shut, and stared hard at Fairfax. At length he said: "'T is the man. I'd swear to him on Tyburn Hill. He hath the same set o' the shoulders, and the same backward carriage o' the head, like one who had ne'er looked on his better."

"Yes, yes," broke in Beverley impatiently; "'t is needless to say more. The recognizance is full and perfect. Now state to the court what took place at Boynton Hall on that night when the papers were stolen."

"What papers?" asked Fairfax, quickly; and ere the prosecutor could protest Boynton answered dully, "Why, Nat. Bacon's commission, of course; you should know, who stole it."

"Ha," cried Fairfax, triumphantly, whilst Berkeley turned red with rage, "was there indeed a commission from the King to Bacon? Then I have nothing further to answer upon this count. 'T were waste of time to tarry on this matter. As I confess to the securing of the King's commission, so I do most freely confess myself to have been in arms; yet do I repel the aspersion of traitor and rebel which hath been cast upon me. What I have done has been in defence of His Majesty's interests. I have fought against the Indians who were slaying the King's servants and despoiling them of their means of livelihood. I have upheld the commission of Nathaniel Bacon, signed by Sir William Berkeley and ratified by act of assembly. When the Governor expressed his confidence in his loyalty and his valor, and when later he did see fit to tax him with 'coward' and 'fool,' and above all, when he took upon himself to hold back the King's commission, 'twas Berkeley, not Bacon, who taxed himself of treason to our Sovereign."

"Enough," cried Ludwell, sternly; "we are not met to listen to the mad attacks of malice and rancor against our Governor and the Chief Justice of this court; but I charge you, gentlemen of the jury, that ye take note of this fellow's words, and carry well in mind what bearing they have upon the second count of this indictment. Is the prosecutor ready to proceed with his witnesses on this head?"

But the words which had been uttered had aroused intense excitement among both jury and spectators, for rumors had for some time been abroad, the truth whereof no man knew, that Berkeley had suppressed a royal commission to Bacon, — something that it would by no means suit the Governor and his adherents to have known, as the prosecutor well understood. His blundering witness was making it too clear, and the ominous murmur in the court-room, as well as Berkeley's look, warned him that this matter must be probed no farther. With the adroitness of his calling he avoided the difficulty. "Thou didst never read this paper, I think?" he said to the witness.

"No, not I," answered Boynton.

"Then," said the prosecutor, "I find that I have no sufficient proof upon this count, and will proceed to the next.

"May it please Your Honors, I have but one witness to this heavy charge; but methinks he will prove all sufficient, and the more so that he was a late companion in arms with the prisoner, and himself a repentant and remorseful rebel pardoned by the Governor's clemency. Call Arthur Thorn!"

At this name, for the first time this day, Penelope Payne put back her veil; and had there been any whose attention was not fixed upon the bar of judgment, he might have observed that the eyes so lately veiled by moisture of pity now blazed with a wrath which burned away tears as the fierce sun of August dries the dewdrops on the blades of summer grass.

"Thou wretch!" quoth she; but none noted her.

Court — "Dost thou know the prisoner?"

Thorn — "I do."

Court — "How long hast thou known him?"

Thorn — "A matter of two years, since ever he came to the country."

Court — "Were you with him in Bacon's army at Gloucester Court House?"

Thorn — "I was."

Court — "Didst ever hear him say aught touching the taking off of Berkeley?"

Thorn — "Ay, I heard him say that Berkeley's death would be the greatest good that could befall the country, since if that came to pass all would unite under Bacon."

Court — "Did ever anything happen particular that made thee believe Fairfax devised himself the taking of the Governor's life?"

Thorn — "There did."

Court — "Tell thy story to the court."

Thorn — "I trust Your Honors will pardon me if my story be over long, for many incidents thereof are fixed in my mind, and I tell it with deep regret, which hindereth me, and plucketh me back from bearing testimony thus against a comrade in arms, and a former friend."

Fairfax gnawed his under lip, as though to be called this man's friend were worse aspersion than the charge of treason and murder.

Court — "Say it at what length thou wilt."

Thorn — "Then, may it please the court, it was

one evening in October last, just before Bacon was taken ill. The sun was fading in the skies, when, chancing to find myself outside the canvas flap of General Bacon's tent, —"

("Eavesdropping as usual," muttered Fairfax under his breath.)

"— I was about to enter; but hearing voices within I paused, fearing my company might be held an intrusion. Even while I halted thus, I saw a black coming out — a black whom I recognized at once as the body servant of Sir William Berkeley, and under his arm he bore a pigeon and a white packet."

Court — "Heard ye anything said?"

Thorn — "Ay, I heard the voice of the prisoner say: "Pompey, here is a half-crown for thee, and I will make it a whole one an these safely reach the one for whom they be intended."

"Being much wrought upon to pluck out the heart of this mystery, I passed in as Pompey passed out, and then I saw the prisoner sitting with his head on his hands, and his brow as gloomy as though he saw the scaffold which that night's work should nail for him."

"A crafty thrust!" groaned Fairfax.

"A dastardly stab in the dark!" muttered Colonel Payne.

"Stepping up to him I said, 'Methinks thou couldst scarce look solemner were there *poison* in your packet.'"

Scarce looking up or seeming to give much heed to who it was spoke, he muttered, "Ay, poison; enough, perchance, to be the spoiling of two lives."

At this a thrill of horror ran through the listeners. The taking off of the Governor might, to a mad fanatic, seem only but a form of warfare; but that he should aim at another, perhaps Lady Berkeley, the innocent to suffer with the guilty, — this were the unpardonable sin.

Angry murmurs began to rise from all quarters:
"Hang him!"
"To the gallows!"
"He should be drawn and quartered."

"Prisoner at the bar," quoth Berkeley, "the evidence against you is grave; have ye any to bring against it? Unhappily my servant Pompey died that same month of October, of the Jamestown fever, else might we have a stronger light on this coil. I, too, was taken down about the same time, and Lady Berkeley."

"Faith," said Ludwell, "this tallies but too well with the words of the witness. Didst thou eat of the flesh of pigeon?"

Berkeley — "Why, birds were most of our meat this autumn; but I recall naught special."

Ludwell — "The case is clear; yet that all may be after the form of law we will hear the prisoner if he hath aught to say."

Fairfax — "Your Honor, I have listened in silence, but not that silence which doth give assent to the words of this witness, which are as cunning a tissue of truth and falsehood as any ever woven out of hell. The words he doth attribute to me I *did* speak."

"He owns it."

"'T is his death warrant."

"I did speak the words," repeated Fairfax, unmoved, "but with no such meaning as he doth impute. 'T is true I desired the death of Berkeley, and I would have shot him to the heart had I met him in fair fight upon the field of battle, — and so I doubt not would any one of you have done to Bacon, — but 't is a far cry from war to murder and from honest powder to base poison."

The prisoner's words were spoken so like a true man that they began to weigh in his favor. But Ludwell sternly bade him keep to the point, and explain, if he could, his words and the packet thereon.

Thus bidden, he opened his lips; but no words

would come. Thrice he essayed, and after the last vain effort he said dryly, "Your Honors, I can say naught, — not because I am guilty, but because it toucheth another as nearly as myself, and I would rather die a thousand times than open the matter here to-day."

Ludwell — "So, 'tis a conspiracy. Think not under such thin varnish of honor thou shalt escape. You see, gentlemen, he hath no defence, and I move that the case be charged and go at once to the jury."

"*I ask to be heard as a witness for the prisoner!*"

At these words, uttered in the soft plaintive tone peculiar to the women of Virginia, there fell upon that room a deep amazement.

"'T is Mistress Payne!"

"Nay, surely not."

"Ay — look at her father!"

Truth to say, Colonel Payne gazed on his daughter as on one suddenly gone mad from stress of excitement; and he would have drawn her away to the door, but she put him gently aside, and stood there like some prophetess of old, the wintry sun shining on the glowing coil of her hair, and her eyes dark with feeling, and showing darker yet against the marble pallor of her cheek.

"Call Mistress Penelope Payne!"

At the words she moved forward as one moves in a dream, conscious, yet profoundly heedless, of all around, till, passing Arthur Thorn, she drew her petticoat slightly aside that it might not touch him. He cringed.

For Fairfax, the light of a mighty love and tenderness shone in his eyes as he gazed upon the vision of an angel suddenly alighted as 't were upon this planet to plead his cause. He never dreamed that it would avail aught; but 't was enough and too much of happiness to see her standing there, his friend, his love, his guardian angel.

"May it please the court," quoth the vision, — her voice, which trembled mightily at first, growing ever clearer and stronger as she went on, — "I ask to be heard, for I have that to say which will set both prisoner and witness in far different light from that wherein they now stand before you. 'T is not an easy task for a maiden to lay bare her heart, yet better so than that an innocent man suffer and all of you stand charged at the last day with bloodguiltiness. I know not the ways of courts, whereby, as it hath looked to me this day, all roads save those that lead to the scaffold are barred; but I do beseech you that ye lend an open ear to the plain tale of an untutored, untrained girl, who hath no other counsellor than her own heart,—for neither to mother, father, nor friend have I disclosed that which I would now lay before you."

At these words Sir William Berkeley, once more something of the true knight he had been before the sulphurous cloud of war hid his better nature, cried out:

"Mistress Payne, say on, and thou shalt be heard; I promise thee the protection of the court, and that thy story shall be attended to with open mind."

"I thank Your Excellency, and I do rely upon the kindness of the court. Know, then, that this Arthur Thorn hath vowed long ago that he would do the prisoner some harm."

"Pish! Pish!" interrupted the prosecutor, "what motive could he have?"

"Silence!" thundered the Governor. "The witness is speaking: let none break in upon her discourse."

"What motive had he?" said Penelope, turning toward the prosecutor and repeating his question with scorn in her voice. "The mean motive of one who loves unworthily, who cares naught for the happiness of her he professes to love, unless it be his own happiness as well, and who would rather see her dead at his feet than wed to another."

The infernal gleam in Thorn's eyes attested the truth of her words, and all who looked on him felt that it was even so.

"Ay, but what other?" questioned Ludwell; and his harsh query fell upon the girl's heart, as the rude hand of the executioner tears away the kerchief from the neck of one about to die by the axe.

The maiden red which had quite forsaken the white cheek now rushed up over cheek and brow till it lost itself in the ripples of her hair; but she flinched not. Moving close to the side of Bryan Fairfax, she laid her hand upon the hand of the almost convicted felon and answered:

"*This* other!"

Thus they stood, like man and wife before God's altar, and the stillness of death fell around them.

"Go on, girl," quoth Berkeley at length, but in a softer tone than he had used that day. Perchance his mind was dwelling on the day when Dame Frances Stevens even thus laid her hand in his, and promised to be his helpmeet, for better, for worse, in joy and in sorrow; and he felt a sudden thrill of human sympathy.

"Ay, give me but time and I will tell all. The love I bear this man is the sad fruit of the bitter roots of strife and hatred. The first time ever my eyes lighted on him was yonder, at Rosemary, whither he came at Bacon's command to bring my mother a prisoner to Green Springs. That day I took an oath that come what might, I would never forgive that deed, nor cease to count the doer of it my foe."

The voice trembled again, but she caught herself bravely and went on: "God forgive the making of the oath rather than the breaking of it, for I had not been two days in his company ere I felt the assurance in my heart that, fight under what flag he might, the heart that beat in his breast was loyal, true, and honorable."

The fickle folk in the audience started a faint cheer, but Ludwell checked them sternly. "All this is mighty pretty," he said, "but it hath precious little to do with the matter o' the poison."

"Ay," echoed Berkeley, suspicion jarring in his tone, "what of the poison? Canst thou, Mistress Payne, cast any light upon that packet?"

"Yes, that can I," answered Penelope, "a light so bright that it shall leave naught hid or in darkness. Your Excellency, Bryan Fairfax, in this last autumn, did, in the disguise of a Dutch trader, visit my father's house at Rosemary; and though I knew him for what he was, I durst make no sign, lest he be taken and shot as a spy; for my father was even then at home on leave of absence from the Governor."

"*Penelope!*" The word broke from the lips of Colonel Payne, and such a world of grief, of shame, of tender reproach were in the tone that the maiden sobbed aloud, — "O Father, forgive me! I ne'er meant any deception towards thee — I pray thee, hear me but to the end."

Mastering her emotions at length, she continued: "When I had escaped to my chamber, and had spread out my letter, I found it filled with sweet and bitter — he loved me — and now, alas, I knew too well that I loved him as well. He prayed me send him some word, some token on which he might hang a thread of hope."

Silence again, and for a moment it seemed she could not go on; yet she did, and more boldly.

"That night came the Governor's servant bearing despatches for my father. I remember he sat late over the candle reading of them. For me, my resolve was taken. Pompey (as Your Excellency knows) was my father's servant, and by him given to you, and from a tiny maid this old servant had known and loved me, and I mind me still how I wept when my father sent him away. But to be brief, I did charge him, by the love of other days, to be my messenger as well as my father's; that he should, as the servant of a poor planter having poultry for sale, find his way to Bacon's camp and make opportunity to see Bryan Fairfax, to whom he should deliver my letter, with a message that he should straightway answer that within by the bearer: and to make it sure of that answer's reaching none but me, I bade Pompey bind it under the wing of my white pigeon, which would find its way home though 't were from New Sweden itself."

Here, at length, was a clew; the onlookers brightened, the jury grew more attentive; but Ludwell and Berkeley only hardened both their hearts and faces. " Perhaps you will give us the spirit of his reply," quoth Berkeley, with more than met the ear in his tone; but he little knew the nature of her he had to deal with if he thought to daunt her thus.

" Nay," she flashed out, " not the spirit alone, but the substance. For mine, 't was brief indeed, and comprised but these words: ' The daughter of Colonel Payne will never wed with a rebel. If thou dost indeed love her, come over to the side of thy Governor and thy King!'"

" Bravely said! Now thou art mine own daughter indeed," quoth Colonel Payne.

" And he, — what said he?" questioned Berkeley.

" My lord, here is his letter."

With trembling hand at these words, the maiden drew from her breast a packet, bound with red ribbon, and Arthur Thorn turned livid as he looked upon it.

Every head bent forward, and every ear was strained to catch the syllables as they fell from her lips while she read: —

"SWEET MISTRESS," — thus it ran, — " Thy letter is like a dagger rubbed with balm, healing even while it hurts. Thou lovest me — 'tis as vain to hide it from me as from thyself; and knowing this, I can trust our future to the white wings of the peace which I see hovering over my poor distraught country. Yes, trust to it as now I trust this note to the white wing of the dove thou hast sent me as a messenger. For the conditions thou wouldst bind me to I can but answer in the words of a better man: 'I could not love thee, dear, so much, loved I not honor more.'

"Thine only and thine ever,
"FAIRFAX."

"We have heard enough, Mistress Payne; you can leave the witness-stand," said Berkeley, filled with wrath over the sympathy written on the faces of all around, and half regretting the protection he had extended to the witness. "Gentlemen of the jury," he concluded, when the public prosecutor had spoken once more, "ye have heard the evidence, — ye have heard how on the first counts the prisoner stands, confessed by his own mouth, guilty as charged. 'T is for you to decide whether one who hath the hardihood, even now, to glory in such deeds were like to stick at the last. A thief, a spy, and a rebel he is, by his own confession; it only remaineth for you to decide whether he did also seek to become a murderer."

The jury left the room, but 't was a short time ere their return brought all eagerly trooping back to their seats in the court. The clerk called the roll while the jury stood.

"Are ye all agreed of your verdict?"

"Yea."

"Who shall say for you?"

"The foreman."

Then said the clerk: "Bryan Fairfax, hold up thy hand. Look upon the jury. Gentlemen of the jury, look upon the prisoner, — is he guilty or not guilty as in the indictment charged?"

"Guilty of bearing arms under Bacon."

Berkeley's eyes flashed with rage. "That is no verdict," he thundered, "and we will not receive it. Is he guilty or not guilty as charged in the indictment? It is not for you to draw distinctions. Retire, and return your verdict in the form in which the law and the court command, or it shall be worse for you."

Again a murmur arose from the spectators, and

the faces of the jury flushed angrily as they withdrew. When at length they came back into court, and the question as to their verdict was asked with the same solemnity as before, they stood with compressed lips and determined faces, and their foreman answered: "Guilty on the first and on the second count, but recommended to mercy."

"How say you of the last counts?"

"*Not guilty.*"

At these words such a cheer shook the house as could have been heard a mile away. It was a cheer, not so much for Bryan Fairfax as for Penelope Payne. But Berkeley liked it none the better for that. It was the first open defiance of his will, and he resented it with all the gall and bitterness of his perverted nature.

Beverley and Ludwell put their heads close, and Ludwell whispered in the Governor's ear: "T' is an infamy to have acquitted him of the well-proven attempt on thy life, but no matter; the treason is clear, — off with him to the gallows!"

But Beverley, perchance through having less in his own person to resent, saw more clearly than his fellows that the temper of the people was not to be tried too far.

"Forget not," said he, "that there are other prisoners to be tried for this rebellion, and it is not wise to thwart too openly a jury drawn from our own friends; besides, remember the coming of the commissioners. Methinks it were well to have one instance of clemency to point to, and all the better that 't were the pardon of an affront to one of his judges, and of the suspicion of a graver offence toward another."

"'T is easy to forgive where we have suffered no injury," sneered Ludwell.

The point of Beverley's argument had penetrated Berkeley's mind. He felt that to press his authority too far was to lose all. Loath as he was to risk, or even to defer his vengeance, caution conquered. "Since you are not agreed, gentlemen," said he, somewhat coldly to Beverley and Ludwell, "I must decide betwixt ye, and I hold Beverley's counsel to lean more to the side of prudence, though methinks Ludwell hath spoken more like true friend of mine. Yet even at the risk of letting the scoundrel escape, 't is safer to temporize. We have him still, and if I have aught to say, the gibbet shall still claim its own."

Having spoken in low tones to his associates, Governor Berkeley rose, and every eye was fixed on him: "Bryan Fairfax," said he, "you are convicted of a heinous offence against the state,— an offence for which the penalty is death. Your judges do accordingly sentence you to stand upon the scaffold at James City from nine o'clock until noon, and afterward to be hanged by the neck till you are dead, — and may the Lord have mercy on your soul."

A rising tide of wrath began to make itself heard, but Berkeley stayed it with his hand as he concluded:

"Yet since the jury hath recommended thee to mercy, we have decided to grant a respite of an hundred days, with ten more added of our grace, wherein you may, if you will, seek pardon of our Sovereign Lord, the King; and," he added, with the same cruel irony with which he had formerly addressed Drummond, "bring to the notice of his advisers the points which your doubtless profound study of the law has enabled you to raise. Wherefore we do grant you reprieve until the twenty-third day of April next."

"Faith," said one to another as the court broke up, "'t is but a refinement of cruelty; for how can news cross and re-cross the ocean in any such space of time, — above all when every vessel is hindered by winter storms?"

But when Penelope Payne heard the words, joy conquered that soul which sorrow could not bend. She grew white, she staggered, she would have fallen, but her father's arms were around her, and his voice whispered in her ear: "My poor child, would I had died ere this befell."

"Did I do wrong, father?"

"Nay, my daughter; 't is no mortal's fault that love conquers him. Methinks thou hast been but the brave maid I would have had thee. Come away. Whate'er comes to thee we will bear it together."

Scarce heeding his words, Penelope murmured over and over, "The King's pardon — I must have the King's pardon!"

"Ay," said Colonel Payne, breathing deep determination, "and thou shalt, or thou and I will die in the seeking of it."

CHAPTER XII.

PENELOPE'S PILGRIMAGE.

> Though seas and lands be twixt us both,
>   Our faith and troth
>   Like separated souls,
>   All time and space controls.
> Above the highest sphere we meet
> Unseen, unknown; and greet as angels greet.

WHEN Penelope left the court-room her mind was set in that heroic key to which danger and difficulty are but a spur and an excitement. She would have faced the rack or the stake without a tremor. But reaction is the inevitable penalty of such exaltation; and in the watches of the night, as she lay in her little white bed in her chamber at Rosemary, her forebodings conjured up lions in her path till her heart sank, but never failed. The sea, the dark, the stormy, the terrible, must be crossed, and alone; for the physician had declared but the other day that her mother's life hung by such an uncertain thread that none could say what day might end it, and 't was clear that her father could not be spared from home.

To be separated from this dear mother in such a season of storm and stress, — what a trial! And perhaps never to look upon her face again, — but from that thought she turned away, as youth has power to do from that which it finds insupportable.

It was agreed between her and her father that she should sail on the "White Lady," which was about to depart, with Captain Bennett, whose wife was but too glad of a companion on the voyage. So far all was clear; but this uncle to whose care she was to be consigned, — what did she know of him? What did even her father know of him save that he had married her mother's younger half-sister, Elizabeth St. Michel, when her grandfather, a French Huguenot, had sought to earn a livelihood in England? From time to time rumors had crossed the water and come to Colonel Payne, that his brother-in-law was a rising man in politics, a faithful servant of the crown, favorably known in the navy office for his shrewdness and diligence; and once a packet had brought from over seas a trunk full of modish gowns and dainty laces, and a high tortoise-shell comb, and a cloak of cramoisie. Penelope remembered to have seen a tear fall from her mother's eye, and to have heard her say, "'T is good of Samuel to have sent me these reminders of Elizabeth;" but she never wore any of them. Penelope had oft pictured to herself the form and face of this dead and gone aunt, who loved laces and cramoisie cloaks, and perfumed jessamine gloves. By the aid of a miniature in her mother's drawer she could easily conjure up the merry, dancing eyes, the dark hair turned over a cushion away from the forehead, and the childish, petulant, pouting, altogether bewitching mouth.

"Had thine aunt but changed her black hair to copper-colored, as I am told the London dames oft do by the aid of dyes, the portrait might pass for one of thee, Penelope." So her father had said to her a year since; and Mistress Penelope, looking in her glass, had sighed and blushed and whispered to herself, "I would I were half as beautiful."

If only this aunt were living, the going over seas (so she thought) would have lost half its terrors; but her uncle seemed far away, a stranger in a strange land, — how would he receive her? How much help could he give her in gaining an audience of the King? *An audience of the King!* Ah, that was the most terrible of all. That she, Penelope Payne, an unfledged, unschooled, provincial maiden, should present herself before a monarch to ask a boon, — sure never since the days of Esther had any undertaken so rash a mission.

One thought alone could sustain her fainting courage, — the vision of that white set face, those arms in bonds, rose before her, and made her ready to brave every peril. "For Bryan's sake," was the motto borne on her breast.

The days came and went, and she heeded not the flight of time. In one place only her heart found peace, — by the bedside of her mother, where peace ever reigned. It had been agreed between her and her father that nothing of her troubles should be brought in to cloud the heavenly atmosphere of that sick room. Her mother knew only that her daughter had offered of her own free will to go over to seek the pardon of those who were under the fatal ban of Berkeley's wrath, and despite all misgivings, she rejoiced in her heart that her child was suddenly grown out of childishness into something high and heroic, beyond her simple ken. It was enough for her that Penelope's father approved her going. Like Luther's little bird, she sat upon the twig of life content, letting God take care.

Colonel Payne wished from his soul that he could share his wife's tranquillity; but each one of the four days which elapsed between the sentencing of

Fairfax and the sailing of the "White Lady" brought him fresh misgivings. His own memories of London, and the tales he had heard of the Court of the Merry Monarch, taught him far more than his daughter could know of possible snares and pitfalls spreading before her unwary feet. More than once, indeed, was he moved to warn her; but ever as he opened his lips, his eye fell upon the face whose radiant transparency revealed the purity of the soul within, and he turned away abashed to hint at wrong. He consoled himself by repeating, when he was alone, the lines from Comus (a masque, which as a youth he had seen acted on the grounds of My Lord, the Earl of Sandwich), and which had made so deep an impression that he was wont sometimes to recite passages as he rode or walked alone. Now he recalled the entry of the rabble rout, the wild orgy, the peril of the lady, and then those comforting words:

> "So dear to heaven is saintly chastity
> That when a soul is found sincerely so
> A thousand liveried angels lackey her,
> Driving far off each thing of sin and guilt."

Yes, to this angelic guidance and guardianship he committed his child, and thereafter he feared less the hour of her setting forth. One whole day he devoted to writing a letter to her uncle, to whose care she was going, — a letter so touching in its simplicity, its manliness, and confident appeal to the claims of kinship, that this distant uncle must have been hard of heart indeed if he softened not to sympathy with this niece come so far on so forlorn a hope. For the further conciliation of his brother-in-law, Colonel Payne gathered together a store of all Virginia commodities, tobacco, and pipes of Powhattan clay, maize dried in the ear, together with such Indian relics as beads, and strings of wampum, and a pearl cap which the Queen of Pamunkey had sent him as a gift. Much ease of mind did the good Colonel find in thus busying himself with trifles, that he might in the crowd of little things forget the great; and finally, there was the drawing up of the petition for pardon, and the securing of signatures, which offered themselves so plentifully that the tribute contained therein sustained Penelope, and even raised within her a sad and painful pleasure. If all the world loves a happy lover, much more does it cherish one whose love has gone awry. Many there were too who would fain have shown her sympathy, but dared not, so deeply stood they in dread of the tyrant in the Governor's chair. The very jailer softened at sight of her sorrow-stricken young face; and while he durst not grant her admission to the prison, he bade her be beneath the barred window at dusk and he would bring his prisoner thither.

The memory of that meeting abode with Penelope Payne to the last day of her life, — the whispered greetings, the hurried exchange of vows, the reluctant farewells, and finally the meeting of the lips through the iron bars. Never was betrothal kiss so sad, so solemn, or perchance (by that strange law of compensation which evens the lot of mortals) so sweet.

All through that last night Penelope felt it tingling upon her lips in all its pain of passionate sweetness. All night the last vows of Bryan Fairfax rang in her ear: "I am not worthy, but I love thee, and living or dying I am thine."

The next morning, the seventh of January, the destined day of her setting forth, dawned grayly. Penelope dressed by candle-light, and watched as in a dream the cording of her chest. After one hurried embrace she tore herself from her mother's fond arms, while still enough mistress of herself to keep back the thick gathering tears.

It was a gloomy day indeed for the undertaking of a journey. The clouds swept scudding across the sky, the trees shook in the blast, and the trunk of a giant pine, felled in last night's storm, lay athwart the road, so that they were compelled to alight and climb over it to reach the dock, the spray blowing in their faces as they passed.

On the deck of the "White Lady" they saw Captain Bennett giving orders to the sailors, and making ready as fast as possible for the start.

"Must ye needs set sail in weather like this?" asked Colonel Payne, as they joined him, having with difficulty come aboard by means of a rude ladder which swayed with the swaying of the vessel.

"Why, 't is no more than we may meet any day in the open sea; no man looks for summer seas in January. I have tarried a week already, hoping for calmer weather. But fear not for your daughter's safety; 't is not for naught that I have sailed the 'White Lady' for nigh on to thirty year in every latitude from the Dutch coast to the Spanish main."

The trouble in Colonel Payne's face did not lighten. Suddenly turning to the maiden at his side, he cried: "Penelope, I cannot let thee go. Tarry at least for the next sailing; another ship is already loading and will set out a week hence."

"Father, say no more, I pray thee. It grieves me sore to try thee thus; but sure thou hast forgot that a man's life is at stake. April is but three months away, and the ocean must be twice crossed. For me I do but count every moment lost that holds me here, and would fain be in among the sailors, hoisting sails and making fast the sheets."

"And has it come to this," said her father with grave sadness, "that a stranger hath so absorbed thine heart that thou hast no room therein any longer for those who of old stood first with thee?"

"Oh, father, father, say not so," cried Penelope, throwing herself into his arms and bursting forth in a tempest of weeping. "Love me, father, for never did I crave thy love so much; and for myself, I feel that I have ne'er before known what love meant. Through my love for Bryan my heart has grown into a deeper love for thee and for my mother. Ah, how hard it is to part from her!"

"There, there," answered Colonel Payne, soothingly, "thou wilt find lions enough in thy path ahead to take up all thine attention, and thou must give as little heed as thou canst to the enemy behind thee. Remember, God stays though thou go, and he will have thy mother in his keeping. Oh, my child, 't is a hard blow to me that her illness keeps me here, and doth compel me to let thee set out thus alone on seas stormier than you in your ignorance can foresee."

"But, father, 't is with the good Captain."

"Ay, child, thou hast said, — the good Captain be thy pilot!"

"Sorry am I to break in upon your parting, Colonel," said Captain Bennett's voice, "but the tide serves, and we must be hoisting anchor. Mistress Payne's chest is in her cabin, and my wife will see to it that she lacks nothing. The box thou art sending to Mr. Pepys is also safe stowed in the hold. Let me see once more; I have his address, methinks, writ here." So saying, he drew from his wallet the slip, from which he read aloud, "Mr. Samuel Pepys, Seething Lane, Crutched Friars, London."

"Ay, 't is the right place unless (which God forefend) he be moved away, now he is out of the Navy Office. I doubt not he will receive ye kindly; for though he was sometimes hasty, he was ever fond of his wife and, for her sake, of her sister, Penelope's mother. Mistress Payne hath ne'er seen her sister since coming to America, yet was the news of her death none the less a blow; for out here the affections, methinks, do but cling the closer to home and home-ties. Penelope hath more of her aunt than her mother in her, which I pray may touch her uncle's heart. Be good to my maid, Captain, and may Heaven reward you!"

The good Captain blinked hard; then he stretched forth his hand heartily.

"She shall be as mine own, Colonel."

The two men gripped hands, then Payne turned to his daughter and gave her one last embrace. "Thou hast the petition safe, child?"

"Ay, father, sewed to my bodice."

"And thy bag of gold?"

"Ay, in the belt around my waist."

"Then must we say farewell; but promise me that whilst thou art gone thou wilt set down, day by day, all that passes, that if ye do hear of a ship coming this way we may have not the hurried words of a last moment, but the free record of each day's thoughts and actions, — 't is for this I have given thee the journal I brought hither at my first coming out of England."

"I fear 't will be but sorry reading; but what thou bidst me, I will faithfully perform so far as in me lies."

"Thou wast ever a good and faithful child."

"And, father, thou wilt in turn strive to send me tidings by the next ship. Remember how my heart will hang on thy words."

"Trust me, — I will not forget; and now, — farewell!"

"Farewell!"

"Farewell!"

As if a thousand farewells could ever speak

the emotions and wishes of those who love and part!

． ． ． ． ． ． ． ． ．

Swiftly down the sullen river dropped the black-hulled ship. On the wind-swept wharf a gray-haired man stood motionless, watching its outlines grow dim and disappear. A great sob swelled in his throat. "My little girl!" he cried; "my little, little girl!"

CHAPTER XIII.

OVER SEAS.

Coelum non animam mutant qui trans mare currunt.

IT often comes to pass that an ill beginning makes a good ending; and so it proved with Penelope's journey. No sooner was the ship "White Lady" outside the harbor of Chesapeake Bay than the wind shifted from easterly to westerly, and a favoring gale bore her so swiftly on her way that Captain Bennett swore a good round sailor's oath that 't was the best trip he had known in a quarter of a century.

To Penelope, lying with closed eyes in her berth, all space and time seemed but one dreary blank, marked off by the tossing of the ship and the beating of the great waves against her side. Whenever she opened her eyes she seemed to see "April — the twenty-third of April!" written in letters of fire before her vision. When she slept, her starts and moans were pitiful to note; and when she woke it was with a sigh, as of one who takes up anew a burden well-nigh too heavy for the shoulders that must bear it.

At length, one night after thirty days' sailing, the Captain's wife, whose long experience at sea had compelled her to be somewhat of a physician, lacking other medical advice, came into the cabin with a sleeping potion, which she bade Penelope swallow, saying, "One good night's rest must thou have, for I should be much ashamed to show thee as thou art now to thine uncle. He would think we had brought him some patient from a Virginia hospital, — nay, perchance a mad-house." The softness of her voice more than atoned for the harshness of her words, and with a sad smile Penelope sat up and swallowed the draught, which soon took such effect that she lay back upon her pillow and fell into a deep, unconscious, restful sleep, which lasted far into the morning. When she woke, she felt herself so refreshed that she was able to creep on deck, where to her great joy and bewilderment she saw a flock of land-birds flying overhead and the great cliffs of England looming up in the blue distance.

It is scarcely possible for any with English blood in their veins to look upon those cliffs for the first time without a deep emotion. 'T is a home-coming even to one born thousands of miles away; for this little island is the homestead of the race, and rich in all the traditions which are very part and parcel of the lives of its children. As Penelope looked upon its still distant shores, a thousand recollections of tales heard in childhood at her father's knee rose in her mind, and for an instant blotted out the insistency of her private trouble. To the soul wearied and harassed by the present there is no balm like that distilled by thoughts of the past. Steeped therein our little lives assume more nearly their true proportion, and unconsciously we find ourselves less at war with Fate. So it proved with this sorrowful young maid. Sitting on a coil of rope upon the deck, with both arms on the rail and her chin propped thereon, she drew in deep draughts of consolation and sustaining power from the broad seas around her and the nearing shores of her father's old home, which seemed to stretch out arms of welcome to her as his child, and to bid her take courage, for that she was coming not among aliens, but to friends and kindred.

In spite of itself youth is beguiled and cheated of its grief by the passing show; and when at the end of another day the "White Lady" had come through the swelling channel and threaded her way into the calm waters of the Thames, Penelope was absorbed in watching the new life about her. To her eyes, accustomed to the broad Virginia rivers, this muddy stream, filled with boats of every sort and size, and spanned by bridge after bridge, seemed so narrow and insignificant that she could scarce believe it was the same Thames which had played so great a part in history, borne pageants on its bosom, welcomed queens, and wafted great men to yonder gate of London Tower which loomed grim above them.

The grating of the ship against her pier, the smell of tar along the docks, the rude song of the sailors, "How! How! Rum below!" as they made fast the ropes which bound her to the dock, the rumbling of carts, the cries of the Thames watermen, and that strange overwhelming roar made up of many indistinguishable sounds and resembling the voice of some live creature, at last forced upon Penelope the consciousness that this was London, and that her journey of three thousand miles was come to an end.

As the full realization swept over her, a great weakness and trembling came upon her; but Mrs. Bennett, whose motherly heart yearned tenderly over the girl in this great sorrow, bade her be of good cheer, for that she and Captain Bennett would never leave her till they had seen her safe in her uncle's charge. Yet at these words her heart failed her still more. "What," she thought "if this Uncle Pepys were dead (for 't is five years since we had word of him, and his health was already breaking then, and he spake of himself as an old man though scarce forty), — what if he believed not my story, and would neither consent to aid nor even to receive me under his roof? What if he were removed to another part of the world and none could tell us whither?"

All of this speculating of poor Penelope's was as idle as hoping and fearing generally are; for nothing fell out according to her foretelling. When the hackney coach, with its burden of people and trunks and boxes drew up before the house in Seething Lane, Crutched Friars, not far from the Tower of London, Mr. Pepys was found to live there, and came down bare-headed to the coach with a bow which Mrs. Bennett judged mighty handsome, considering she had given him no clew as to who it was he was about to receive, only sent in word that two ladies would fain speak with him at the door. As her uncle stood thus uncovered by the coach window, Penelope, who was at the further side, had full opportunity to study him while herself unobserved. She scanned him eagerly, though her heart was beating so hard it well-nigh choked her, and a sort of mist gathered before her eyes.

What she saw was a very proper, gentlemanlike person, in attire which to her provincial eyes appeared extraordinarily fine, being of drab-colored camelot, very rich, and enlivened by a waistcoat of flowered tabby velvet. His hands were very white, and he held them before him from time to time as though he loved them, and found much satisfaction in their smooth nails and taper ends. His face was large; so large that the expression thereof could scarce cover so vast an expanse, and there were spaces vacant of meaning. The cheeks bagged somewhat over the falling band of plaited lawn, and the nose was a trifle red and swollen at the end, as though dipt too often in Canary. But as if to balance these defects, the forehead was both smooth and high under the curls of the wig, and the eyes twinkled with good sense and good humor.

"I bid you welcome, ladies," he said graciously, as he assisted Mrs. Bennett and her charge to alight; which was surely gracious since he knew not yet who they were.

When they had come in and sat down in the withdrawing room, Mrs. Bennett drew forth the letter from Colonel Payne and bade Mr. Pepys read it, that he might discover for himself the reason and the purport of this intrusion.

Taking the packet with another handsome bow, he answered, "By your leave, ladies, I will withdraw to my study while I read this, for mine eyes are growing weak, and the light of candles at the play last night went near to put them quite out. I must therefore seek aid from my eye-tubes to make this writing plain."

Scarce had he left the room ere Mrs. Bennett burst forth in his praises. "A proper man, my dear, a very proper man, — as fine a suit as I e'er saw yet, and Captain Bennett hath touched at thirty-seven ports since we were married. I doubt not his heart is as good as his legs, — and they would do credit to any man. Yes, good legs bespeak the gentleman. I am glad he is a gentleman. I could ne'er have borne to leave thee with one who was less."

Thus the good woman ran on in that belief cherished by so many that people in trouble must be talked to without ceasing, as those in danger of freezing are walked up and down.

For the moment Penelope was far more concerned to know what Mr. Pepys thought of her than what she thought of him, and she was mightily uneasy in her mind till his return. But his smile, as he re-entered the room, did much to reassure her; and coming up very kind, he took her hand,

and, looking at her close, he said: "So this is the child of Theophilus Payne, and my wife's half-sister Alice. And your name is Penelope? Well, Mistress Penelope, I am mightily pleased to see you, and I will do what I can for you, as your father desires. I fear 't will be but little I can do, for Samuel Pepys is sadly out of favor at court; but for my wife's sake I will make the trial. Meanwhile, have in the chests, and I will bid Betty set in order a chamber for your reception; for since the death of my wife the blinds have scarce been opened over half the house. I count it ill done that the sun should fade the furniture when there be none to tread thereon, and the hangings in this room alone did cost me three pound six."

"I make you my compliments, Mr. Pepys, on your economy and good management," said Mrs. Bennett. "But can it be that ye are your own housekeeper?" Under all her simplicity the Captain's wife was a woman of much shrewdness and knowledge of the world, and she hoped to find some older woman than the apple-cheeked maid who had opened the door, in charge of the household. Great, therefore, was her relief of mind when Mr. Pepys answered, "No; I do keep a housekeeper, one Mrs. Fane, who will be in some sort of charge of this young lady. I do not believe that a more knowing, faithful, or vigilant person, or a stricter keeper at home (which to me is a great addition), — a person more useful in sickness as well as health, — can be found anywhere. As such I do much esteem her, and should long desire her neighborhood." This he said in a full, round voice, which might well have reached to the housekeeper's room; then, in a tone judiciously lowered, he added, "But she hath a height of spirit, captiousness of humor, and noise of tongue, that of all womankind I have hitherto had to do withal do render her conversation and comportment most insupportable."

"Poor Penelope!" whispered Mrs. Bennett. "Yet fear not; thou, if any, canst win her over, and after all, 't is for the best — oh, yes, decidedly for the best, my dear — I would not have had it otherwise."

Poor Penelope indeed! Never had she felt her heart so cling to the good Captain, and even to his talkative wife, as now when they rose to take leave.

"Cheer up, my maid," said the Captain, in a low voice, shaking out his colored handkerchief and blowing his nose that he might find excuse for wiping his eyes; "remember that the 'White Lady' lies at the dock yonder, and you have friends there, should all others fail you."

Penelope pressed his big, strong hand, but could trust her voice to utter no word, either to him or to his wife, as she tenderly embraced her.

At last the parting was over, and Penelope had climbed the stairs and found herself in a pretty chamber with an overhanging window looking out upon the busy street,—a window whose tiny diamond panes were set in sashes of stout oaken wood. The bed was covered with a spread of Indian chintz, which, as Betty was at pains to inform her visitor, was made out of the gown worn by Mistress Pepys at the celebration in honor of the coming of Queen Catherine from Spain and her entrance into London. Out of the chamber opened one still smaller, scarce more than a closet, wherein a cot was made for Dolly, whose black skin and gorgeous turban half terrified and wholly amazed the lively Betty.

When Penelope had smoothed her hair and bathed her red eyes with lavender water, that she might not offend her uncle's sight with the traces of her grief (for instinct told her that he was one more like to be moved by charm than by pathos), she bade the maids uncord her chest.

"At what hour does my uncle dine?" she asked of Betty, who answered:

"At three at this time o' year, to save candles;

but he bade me say 't was put off till four to-day that you might have time to make ready."

"Alas!" thought Penelope, "I never counted on this, and I know not what gown to don. Mine uncle dines alone?"

"Yes, Mistress, all alone."

"Then, Dolly, lay out the puce-colored damask with the white cuffs and the muslin whisk. Nay, nay," she added, as Dolly strove to tempt her by holding up a flowered brocade with cramoisie stomacher. "The sad heart cannot brook going gayly clad. I must crave mine uncle's patience with my soberness without and within."

When she was dressed, finding that it wanted still a half-hour of dinner-time, she set herself to making her room more home-like by setting out upon the table her little worn Bible, the journal wherein her father had bade her write, and the miniature of her mother close by the bed, that her eye might rest on it the last thing at night and the first in the morning. Then, summoning all her resolution, she passed out at the low door, and down the winding stair into the study, where her uncle had bade her seek him.

At the moment she entered Betty announced the serving of dinner, and her uncle conducted her with much ceremony to the dining-room. Little zest had Penelope for the feast which had been prepared in honor of her arrival. The pullets, the dish of marrow, the pasty of larks, and the prawns and cheese over which her uncle smacked his lips, were but sawdust to her taste, though she strove to swallow something, that Mr. Pepys might not think her ungrateful for the honor done her; but she soon discovered that the dinner was ordered as much for his own gratification as for hers. The rich dishes put him in excellent humor, and as he sipped his pale ale his soul expanded into confidence. "Yes," he said, leaning back, that his digestion might have the more room, — "yes, you do be of a surety mightily like to your aunt as she was when I married her, and if your eyes belie you not you have a temper very like also. Nay, color not with vexation! — a temper is not so bad a thing in a handsome woman. Your aunt was a good soul for all hers. She is a great loss to me."

"Ay, uncle," answered Penelope, swift tears of sympathy springing to her eyes as she thought of his loneliness, "I can well credit it."

"Yes," he continued, "there be none can cook a pasty like her; and for the preparing of marrow-bones, Betty is a fool beside her. This dish to-night was spoiled."

For the first time in a month Penelope was

inclined to smile at the ending of this speech, so different to that on which she had counted; but she strove to keep a grave face, and replied: "Perhaps the fault lies in thine indisposition, since all do seem to me excellent well prepared, and most orderly set out; and sure no serving-maid could be defter than Betty."

"Betty? — oh, she is well enough, but not to hold a candle to Deb. Now there was a wench — but that is an old tale and not meet for young ears."

"Well, Uncle Pepys," said Penelope, not knowing how to take the turn of the talk, "if it please you to tempt your appetite with variety, I would be right glad to try a new dish for thy breakfast, — a hoe-cake, such as the black servants at home do make of the Indian corn and bake in the ashes."

"I do perceive that thou art a clever lass," answered Mr. Pepys, with more heartiness than he had yet shown, and bestowing a pinch on the ear, — a salute which marked his special approbation. But he said little more, and very soon lighted her candle and bade her get to bed, that she might not miss her beauty sleep.

When Penelope had retired for the night, having put out her candle and said her prayers on her knees, like the pious girl she was, she fell to thinking of the events of the day, and felt that she had much to be thankful for in having found a safe shelter and a kind reception. She was, it is true, disappointed that her uncle had not seen fit to open the subject of her mission, but she saw, or thought she saw in him, a vein of diplomacy, and a disposition to reach home by the longest way round for the mere pleasure of the journeying. "He is fain to study me," she thought, "that he may know how much of weight he may hang on my story," — which, to my thinking, was rather shrewd for a little colonial maiden but one day in London.

CHAPTER XIV.

THE LIONS OF LONDON.

"An exact diary is a window into his heart that maketh it."

"FEBRUARY y^e 14 (Lord's Day) up and to church with mine uncle, but my hart was too hevvy to pay much heed to the discoarse."

Let not the highly educated young woman of the nineteenth century mock at this, the first entry in Penelope Payne's diurnal, — a little worn, brown-covered book, which to-day lies in the closet of an old Virginia country house. The maiden who traced the faint and often illegible lines had never known the guidance of dictionary or grammar, but her heart was as true as though she had spelled it with an "e" instead of without, and on that Lord's Day morning, in the year 1677, no fairer face looked out from beneath its bonnet on an untried world.

The church to which they bent their steps was St. Olave's, hard by Mr. Pepys's house in Seething

Lane; and when the service was done, her uncle took Penelope by boat to St. Margaret's at Westminster, that she might see the marriage certificate of "Samuel Pepys of this parish, Gent & Elizabeth De St. Michel of Martins in the ffields, spinster." Penelope remembered the charming, pouting, smiling face in the miniature at home, and sighed. To youth the dead seem to have been always dead, and it is with a shock that it comes upon such tokens that they, too, once moved and loved, and suffered, as full of life as itself.

To while away the time till dinner should be ready, Pepys and his niece next betook themselves to the Abbey, where Penelope's awe greatly amused good Mr. Pepys, who never felt awe at anything. Even now, as they stood before a richly carved tomb, he chuckled to himself, — "Look," he said, "It is the tomb of Queen Catherine of Valois. You must know, niece, that some years ago I chanced to be in the Abbey when they were opening the coffin of this queen, and, as I was requested to hold the head, I did kiss her mouth, reflecting upon it that it was my birthday, thirty-six years old, that I did first kiss a queen."

Penelope could scarcely restrain a shudder. As she turned away her head in the effort to hide a sudden wave of repulsion, she noticed a gentleman on the other side of the aisle bowing to her uncle; but he having left his eye-tubes at home took no note of him.

"See, uncle," she whispered, "some one yonder is nodding and smiling at us."

At the words Mr. Pepys puckered up his eyes as if hoping thus to screw them into focus, and then of a sudden cried out: "A pox upon me if it be not Mr. Dryden!"

At this a mighty wonder fell upon Penelope, and a deeper awe than the arches of the Abbey had struck into her heart; for the fame of the poet had crossed the seas, and she had heard her father say he had rather meet the great Mr. Dryden than any man in England, — except, of course, His Majesty. So overcome was Penelope, therefore, at this encounter that she could find no fitting words to speak when her uncle presented her as his little savage from the western wilderness of Virginia. Perhaps if she had not known he was a genius, she might not have admired this sallow face with its long nose and thick lips, and least of all the brown warts which stood out from his cheek like toadstools; but it was the face of Mr. Dryden, and that was enough.

He held some jesting talk with Mr. Pepys, asking him if he was come hither to seek convivial companionship in the tombs because the coffee houses were closed by the King's orders; to which Mr. Pepys made neat answer, that he had oft met with men dead drunk, but never any drunk dead.

"Ah, Mr. Pepys," said the poet, offering his snuff-box, which was of carved ivory rimmed with gold, and half shutting his eyes, as was his wont when he talked, "ye have a lively wit and a ready tongue. For me, my conversation is slow and dull, my humor saturnine and reserved. I know not how in conversation to break a jest or frame a repartee."

"Nay, that is but natural," answered Pepys, striving to conceal his gratified vanity. "Your mind is filled with gold pieces, stamped with the image of the Sovereign; but mine is taken up with small change, which doth drop more jinglingly from the tongue, yet, taken all together, hath naught to be compared, in value, with one word of yours."

"Mr. Pepys, you do me too much honor," answered his companion; and then, after some moments of idle and profitless discourse, bowing and scraping like two dancing masters, they parted

"How dull his talk is for a great man!" whispered Penelope, when Mr. Dryden was out of hearing. "To my thinking, you were the better of the two."

White Aprons.

"My dear," said Pepys, "the man will never waste a clever speech by giving it away with his tongue when his pen can sell it for sixpence. Poets cannot afford clever talk. To measure a great man, you must use the yardstick of his public work, not his private walk and conversation."

Penelope was destined to repent her harsh judgment; for that afternoon when dinner was finished, Betty, the maid, came in fetching a bottle of wine for Mr. Pepys, and for his niece a present of a starling in a gilded cage, together with a billet tied with a blue ribbon, wherein, when it was opened, were two stanzas signed with the name of John Dryden, and addressed

"TO THE FAIR STRANGER."

And thus they ran:

"Your smiles have more of conquering charms
Than all your native country arms.
Their troops we can repel with ease,
Who vanquish only when we please.

"But in your eyes — Oh, there's the spell.
Who can see them and not rebel?
You make us captives by your stay,
Yet kill us if you go away."

Penelope's heart fluttered like the starling in her hand. The reference to the rebellion in Virginia in the first verse was almost too much for her firmness. The writer little knew on how sore a wound his light words would fall, and, for the flattering lines to herself, it was past her power to comprehend them, and she handed them over to her uncle, who looked first at the wine, then at the bird, then at the verses, and at length burst out a-laughing.

"Faith," said he, "I had quite forgot 'twas Valentine's Day. Pretty well, Mistress Pen, for your first week in London! The laureate of England, it seems, would fain have thee for his Valentine, and this bottle of old Madeira is for the go-between, Samuel Pepys."

With this he fell a-laughing again, till poor Penelope, blushing and quite overcome, ran away to her chamber with her bird and her billet. Sooth to say, so untaught was her mind that the verses seemed to her a little — just a little — silly, though she would never have owned as much. For the starling, he was both a joy and a sorrow, since he put her in mind of the dear woods at home, full of feathered songsters, and also — alas! — of another poor prisoner behind iron bars.

The next morning she woke to the blithe note of the bird and a room flooded with sunshine, and something of the blitheness and the brightness

White Aprons.

found their way to her sad heart; so it was with a lighter heart than she had yet borne that she entered the breakfast-room.

"Give you good morrow," said her uncle. "Have ye forgot the hoe-cake ye did promise to bake for my breakfast?"

"Nay, dear Uncle," answered Penelope; "Betty has ground the corn to meal in the hand-mill and Dolly is even now a-mixing of it, and if you wish I will bake it here before the fire on a board, that ye may see how we do prepare it in Virginia."

Dolly appeared at the door shortly, with a pan of dough made from the yellow meal, and Penelope, taking it from her hand, set it before the blazing fire. As she knelt thus with her back to the room, she was startled to catch of a sudden the sound of a stranger's voice.

"Good morrow, Mr. Pepys," said the voice. "Look not so amazed to see me abroad thus early. I own my repute for idleness doth warrant some surprise at such unwonted hours, but I did much desire to see you on the matter of a navy record which closely toucheth mine affairs. The maid told me I should find you alone." At this instant he became aware of the presence of Penelope, who had turned about, blushing with shame, to be caught thus with her hair ruffled, her sleeves rolled back to the elbow, and her face red with the heat of the fire.

As she lifted her eyes they fell upon a gallant whose every movement and gesture proclaimed the Court. His presence seemed to fill the little room; and as the sunlight flashed upon the shoe-buckles set with brilliants, and the single amethyst which formed the cover of his pouncet-box, he looked for all the world like the prince in a fairy-tale. His eyes were half-closed, as though he saw nothing in the world worth opening them for; but between their lids glittered a line of light which made their laziness a perjury. The face was a delicate oval, the nose somewhat over-large but well formed, like the lips beneath it, which were partly covered by a streak of mustachio so flat, so straight, and so black that it put Penelope in mind of the strips of sticking-plaster which Lady Berkeley wore in the shape of a bow on her cheek at the Governor's Ball.

The girl stood still looking upon him, attracted by his beauty, yet repelled by a certain something (she herself could scarce have said what) which underlay all this grace and elegance.

The unannounced visitor stood still likewise, staring hard at Penelope; then bursting into a noisy and insolent laugh, he lunged forward and cried out to the master of the house, giving him at the same time a prodigious dig in the ribs with his bejewelled knuckles, " Pepys, ye old sinner, whom have ye in hiding here?"

Mr. Pepys crinkled up his puffy eyes and pursed up his mouth as if he were about to burst into a loud haw-haw; but catching his niece's look of mingled indignation and surprise, he drew himself up and answered with something very near dignity: —

"Your merriment, my Lord, is ill-timed, and you are to seek in respect. This lady is Mistress Penelope Payne, niece to my late wife, and but recently come hither from Virginia to try if she may secure the King's pardon for one apprehended in arms under Bacon, — a friend of her father, and one that hath done him great service; by name, Bryan Fairfax."

"How, a Fairfax!" cried the guest, as if glad of an occasion to turn the subject of talk. "Belike 't is some cousin of my wife; for of all the sons of Adam, I dare be sworn more than half do bear her name. I must look into the matter; and meanwhile may I crave the honor of being presented to Mistress Payne?"

His manner was now so different from that with which he first spoke that Penelope could scarcely believe it was the same man; but her uncle called her to his side: "Niece," he said, "I would have thee acquainted with a great gentleman of the Court, His Grace, the Duke of Buckingham."

Penelope courtesied as low as she dared on the slippery floor, but her soul was too set on its purpose to lend aught of timidity to her manner.

"Of the Court, saidst thou, uncle?" she repeated with an innocent, childlike upward gaze, wide-eyed and trustful. "Then perchance he will tell us how best to reach the ear of His Majesty."

Again the stranger fell a-laughing, but with more softness and civility than before. "Ye must know, young lady," he said, stroking back with his long fingers the lace about his wrists, lace so old and rare that it could only have been found among the looted treasures of some convent,—"ye must know that I am but recently come from a retirement of some months' duration in the sequestered shade of London Tower, where if I would have communicated with the King I must needs have done it through the gentleman usher of the Black Rod. Truth to tell," he added, speaking to Pepys rather than to his niece, "my present favor with His Majesty is like a basket of eggs, and must be carried with nicety else all is spoiled. So far from seeking any boon, my one thought by night and by day is how I may do the King some service or secure him some new diversion."

At this he broke off and stared at Penelope till her cheeks began to wax hot; then of a sudden he continued: "Pepys, I see a light, — I see a light. The King holds Court at Whitehall soon."

"Ay," answered Pepys, "but I am little like to profit by that, for I have writ thrice begging the privilege to come kiss the royal hand, and each time the answer is 'Not yet.'"

"Why, then, we are both in the same boat; yet if Beauty guides the helm 't is not impossible we may both sail full into the eye of the King's favor."

At this he turned and made Penelope another bow, so low that the powder from his enormous periwig whitened the floor. Her uncle too turned, and seemed to study her with attention. Then he shook his head, — "Nay," said he, "we covet not the honors of the house of Castlemaine. There be some royal favors bought too dear."

"Trust me," quoth the Duke; "I mean naught of that sort, but only that by helping this fair damsel in distress I might help mine own cause as well, — and for the matter o' that, if the pardon be for a Fairfax, 't is a family cause I do espouse."

Mr. Pepys looked but half convinced, but the Duke rattled on as though all were settled. "I will see to it sure that you receive a mandate to bring your fair niece to Court, and then her own eloquence must do the rest, though I do heartily proffer her my poor services."

"I trust," he added, with a languishing glance out of his sleepy eyes at Penelope, "that as you have been so short a time in this country no man has been before me to claim you as a valentine, and that this felicity and favor may fall upon me."

"I most humbly thank your Grace," said Penelope, courtesying once more, "but yesterday Mr. Dryden did me the honor to ask the same."

"So, so," laughed his Grace, yet with a little testiness, "Master John is in the field a'ready, is he? By the Lord, 't will be fine sport to have him for a rival, for he hateth me roundly, as I hear."

"For what cause, my Lord?"

"Why, you must know that the poet is as thin-skinned as a new-born lamb, and doth shiver if the slightest breath of ridicule blow on him. Well, one night at the Haymarket I chanced to sit in the box near the stage when one of his plays was on. Nell Gwynne (or Madam Ellen, as the King bids her be called now) was a-spouting in her best manner, with a prodigious deal of tragedy, clapping her hand to her heart, which she had just pretended to pierce with a bodkin, this touching line, —

"'My wound is great because it is so small.'

"The occasion was too fair, and not to be resisted; so, rising in my place and rolling my eyes as far upward as hers, I cried out, —

"'Then 't would be greater were it none at all!'

"The pit roared, and the house was set in such a commotion of merriment that the manager was forced to draw the curtain, and the play hath never since been set on."

"Faith," quoth Pepys, laughing, as none could help, so droll was the burlesque of his imitation, "methinks a less peevish poet than Mr. Dryden might be vext to see his lines so rendered before his eyes. But now we will to our business, — these navy records, touching which I have twice this week writ the Duke of York."

Perceiving that her uncle wished to be left alone with his visitor, Penelope withdrew to the study, where, in the deep window-seat behind the curtain, occupying her fingers over a piece of tapestry, she strove to stitch away the tumult of her grief and anxiety. Betty brought her breakfast on a tray; but the hoe-cake was burned to a crisp, and Penelope could have wept, while her cheeks were hot with blushes, fearing her uncle and the Duke had made merry over Virginia fare.

An hour or more slipped away. She heard her uncle enter and begin to busy himself over his papers; but her thoughts were three thousand miles away, and she heeded him not, nor yet the opening of the door, nor the maid's announcement of "Mr. John Dryden."

She was gathering her stitchery and working materials and making ready to come forward; but before she appeared, the gentleman remarked that he was come to inquire after his valentine, and straightway launched into such a eulogy as brought the blushes thick and fast to Penelope's cheek.

She had no courage now to present herself, and was forced to tarry, eavesdropping. She could tell from the sound of her uncle's voice that he was well pleased as he answered: "Ay, ay, Penelope is a fair, comely maid, and like to have as many suitors as her namesake of old. My Lord of Buckingham hath called on me this morning, and, seeing her by chance, he swears he will have her for his valentine. Methinks a damsel that hath captured a Duke and a Laureate within the one week bids fair to run a pretty rig."

"The Duke of Buckingham is a dangerous man, Mr. Pepys, — a very dangerous man."

"Ay, he hath his faults."

"Every man hath faults, but Buckingham alone hath mastered the whole volume of vice."

"Yet he hath a kind heart, and as pretty a wit as any in England."

"Wit? — hm! — if you call it so," — said the poet, tapping his pouncet-box impatiently; "I would name it rather buffoonery. Heard ye of the scene when he drove my play from the stage?"

"Yes, I did catch some hint thereof."

At this Penelope fancied she could hear a tone of vexation in the poet's voice as he cried out, —

"God grant I die not till I have written our controversy!"

"Say rather till ye have *righted* it," said his host, smoothly; but Mr. Dryden would not be appeased.

"Pepys," said he, "for that ye are a close-mouthed man I will read ye some lines from a poem of mine not yet published, and ye shall tell me if it setteth not forth the Duke. Listen, here he stands."

Here Penelope heard the crackling of paper unfolded, and then, after a slight cough to clear his throat, the poet's voice once more reading, —

> "A man so various that he seemed to be
> Not one, but all mankind's epitome;
> Stiff in opinions, always in the wrong;
> Was everything by starts, and nothing long;
> But in the course of one revolving moon,
> Was chymist, fiddler, statesman, and buffoon."

To Penelope's thinking it would have been more true and manly had her uncle spoken out to protect the absent; but he said little, and that little of doubtful interpretation.

When Mr. Dryden had gone and Penelope came out from her enforced hiding, her Uncle Pepys tweaked her ear and called her a sly puss, hiding that she might hear her own praises; but when he saw that tears stood in her eyes he told her that he but jested, and that he did not on the whole feel sorry that she should thus have had a chance to catch a glimpse behind the scenes and be witness of the petty jealousies which afflict the great.

For Penelope it made her rejoice the more that her life had been spent among folk who knew little of such envy and emulation, but lived in simplicity of heart and mind, and save for these late dreadful days of strife, in mutual love and kindliness.

CHAPTER XV.

THREE LETTERS.

"Ah, Love, could thou and I with fate conspire
To grasp this sorry scheme of life entire,
Would we not shatter it to bits, and then
Remould it nearer to the heart's desire?"

THE rain was drizzling outside Penelope's window when she awoke next morning. The fog was settled down so thick she could scarcely see the other side of the street, and she was forced to light her candle that she might see to smooth her hair. It being still too early for breakfast when she was dressed, she drew forth her journal and wrote in much lowness of spirit: "A doleful day, and one wherein naught of good is like to befall. I wold it were away and me one day nearer home."

Seldom are our predictions, even for the short space of a day, borne out by events. We leap up joyously to greet coming happiness, and sorrow lays its heavy hand on our bounding heart and says, "Be still." We rise reluctantly, and set our teeth to bear what the day may bring forth, and lo, happiness and pleasure circle round us, smiling away with gentle irony our fears and our inquietude. So it proved with Penelope. While she was still writing, Betty, the maid, knocked at her chamber door and brought in three letters. Penelope's heart beat fast, for it took her no long time to see that they were from over seas, and that the seal of two out of the three bore the crest of her house. She hugged them to her heart, and kissed the wax again and again.

A second glance showed her the dear and familiar writing of her father and the fine tracing of her mother's hand, now, alas, trembling and fainter than her wont. Which think you she opened first?

Why, God forgive her, it was neither, but the third letter, with superscription written in a bold character, which her eyes had lighted on but once before; but she knew it for the mate of the one her bird had brought her beneath his white wing,— the one borne even now on her heart.

With trembling eagerness she tore it open and read the last words first, — "Thy true lover, Bryan Fairfax." It was enough. He lived. He loved her. For the rest she could wait, and she turned again to the other letters.

Her mother's note, written from her sick bed, was as brave, as cheery, and as full of thought for others as her heart ever was. All her grief, all her anxiety, was for Penelope. It was such a letter as Christiana might have sent back from Beulah-land to her child still struggling up the hill of difficulty.

Her father's letter, too, was one to strengthen the weakest heart: "Be not dismayed, dear daughter," so he wrote; "let us bravely do that which lies in our power, and leave the issue in the hands of that God who hath overruled tyrants greater than Berkeley in the interest of those weaker than we. The King's Commissioners are come, and many be called before them for the giving of testimony; yet they say they bring no instructions to override the Governor, but only to make report upon his administering of his office to His Majesty. There is a bitter quarrel on betwixt Berkeley and Sarah Drummond, from whom he hath alienated the estate of her husband, and turned her and her little ones out of house and home to wander shelterless in the woods but for the kindness and charity of her neighbors. Dame Drummond vows she will have back her property, and is raising heaven and earth to get her case before the King. I know not what the outcome will be. God knows matters look black all around us, and our own dark enough; but I am doing my utmost with Berkeley, and I have striven diligently with Sir John Berry, who hath come over at the head of the Commission, and who at my urgency hath promised to plead the cause of Fairfax with Sir William. Do not despair, therefore, even shouldst thou fail to reach the ear of the King. I have writ your uncle. Should he succeed in procuring for you an introduction at Court, bear in mind my parting words. Put not too much trust in any man — not even in "— (Here certain words were blotted and half scratched out; but Penelope's curiosity leading her to study them the more closely, she could have sworn she read "the King himself," but the matter was beyond her comprehension.)

"Bear thyself," he continued, "like a true and virtuous woman, and thou shalt have no cause to fear snares or pitfalls, though I am told they do mightily abound at Court. Wherever thou goest, my blessing and thy mother's is ever with thee. Forget not, I charge thee, how our good preacher, the worthy Dr. Fuller, hath said there is a tree in Mexicana so tender that if a man but touch its branches it do presently wither away, and that a woman's credit is of equal nicety. I speak this, not that I have not full confidence in thee, but as knowing too well the poison that lurketh in the air of

Courts. Thy dear mother hath failed a little since thy going, but spite of all she is as ever the life and soul and sunshine of the house. She talks and thinks of nothing but thee, and prays ever for thy success. If the prayers of the saints availed in times of old, why not now? Be of good cheer, therefore, and go forward in full faith and with unshaken confidence. I have succeeded through one of the jailers in getting for thee a line from Fairfax, which, methinks, will do more to cheer thee than all the pages I can write. It goes with mine on the ship which sails to-morrow. Who would have thought I could e'er be reconciled to such a marriage for thee! But now my earnest prayer is that God may keep him for thee and send thee safe home to him and to us." (Here a tear blotted the paper.) "He is a fine fellow, and there do be much talk of his cheerful courage in the prison at James City."

Could anything have made Penelope love her father more it would have been these words. "Oh, how unworthy," she thought, "am I of so much affection!"

Having smoothed out this letter and laid it by the side of her mother's, Penelope again took up that other, and having kissed and cried over the outside, she unfolded it slowly and laid it open on her knee.

She felt in that instant the fulness of joy, and was ready to swear that should darkness and sorrow shut down like a mourning veil about her future, this one moment would atone for all.

"My dear Love,"— thus the note began, —" Waste no tears from those bright eyes of thine in thinking upon me. Thy love has made me the happiest man in Virginia; ay, and the proudest, though iron bars be around me and a scaffold before me. Should the worst come, say to thyself, 'There died a man who had known the chiefest good which can come to mortals and whose heart went singing in its prison.'

"Ay, dearest, and 't is not my heart alone that sings, but my voice also, till the gaolers do oft put in their heads, thinking, I verily believe, that through my misfortune I am gone daft. The tune that does be oftest on my tongue is that one you sang in the hall of Rosemary (ah, I can see thee yet, darling, with the September sun glistening in thy bright hair, and the tender look in thine eyes ere my rude summons called the darkness of anger into them), and the burden of those words, — shall I e'er forget them ? — 'Love will find out the way — Love will find out the way!' Ay, doubt it not, dear heart. Not, perchance, the way thou and I in our mortal shortsightedness would choose, but the way which, though it leads through the very Valley of the Shadow of Death, is filled with light and gladness because it is the way of love.

"Till death — ay, and after, — thy true lover,

"Bryan Fairfax."

It was long before Penelope could cease reading this letter over and over; and even when she had conned every word by heart she still pored over the written lines, till Betty knocked once more, to say that Master Pepys was impatient for her coming, and Mrs. Fane was angry that the breakfast was kept waiting so long on the table.

More alarmed at the prospect of Mrs. Fane's wrath than of her uncle's impatience, Penelope hastily tucked away her precious letters, and tripped down the stairs as if her lightness of heart had lent lightness to her feet. Her uncle looked at her quizzically as she entered. "So, Mistress Pen," said he, "you and your father did fancy yourselves a match in state-craft for Samuel Pepys, who hath been near the Court these twenty years. If 't were not so childish simple, one might well be vext thereat."

"How mean you, uncle? Sooth, I am guilty of no deceiving."

"Faith," cried Pepys, slapping his knee, "your ingenuous father writes me that he thinks himself to seek in frankness that he wrote me not upon your first coming that this Bryan Fairfax was your lover as well as his friend, — oh, mighty confidence — deep secret indeed! As if I were like to believe those downcast looks and heart-rending sighs were all for thy father's friend, or that thy father would e'er have given his consent to thy making of thy perilous journey without the occasion was most pressing and personal in its nature! Sooth, I never could have forgiven either him or you but that I knew the convicted rebel was your lover.

"Nay, nay, redden not, nor let fall those tears upon that fresh front of thine, for the laundering thereof will cost sixpence. 'T is no crime to have a lover, — still less to strive to save his life. Now sit ye down, and have a bite of this toasted cheese which Mrs. Fane did prepare because ye did say ye liked it. I know not how ye have twisted that old woman about your pretty finger, but an ye do as well with the King ye may look to succeed without a struggle. 'T is most unfair that youth and good looks should win with ease where plain age must work so hard."

It was evident that Mr. Pepys was in high good humor; but when Penelope asked him tremblingly if he had heard aught touching an audience with the King, he shook his head and counselled her to wait patiently, for that was the first lesson learned at Court. With this, and a tweak of the ear, he bade her fetch her hood and make ready to go out with him, for the rain was clearing, and he was fain to take her with him to the house of a friend.

For this expedition Penelope donned a black paragon petticoat with her aunt's cramoisie bodice, and a whisk of snowy lawn above it, and over all her brown camelot cloak with hood and veil, and, thus equipped, she set forth with her uncle obediently, though with no great interest.

When they were come to the rooms of Godfrey Kneller, who was the friend they were to see, the painter had gone out for a time; but the servant bade them enter and await his coming, which they did. The rooms were warm, and Penelope was glad to accept her uncle's permission to put off her cloak and hood, which he gallantly took from her hand and threw over the high back of the oaken chair whereon she sat beneath the latticed window.

Her uncle was quite right in his assurance that change of scene was the best help for her uneasy soul, and that no anxiety in youth can wholly obscure the interest which lies in novelty. His wisdom showed itself still further in his leaving her now to herself, unmolested by calls upon her attention. But this was, perhaps, as much out of regard for himself as for her, since he was not above taking his own comfort into consideration.

Picking up a volume of Marlowe's plays, he sat down in the corner and began to read, with such absorption of interest that his chuckles and strange grimaces and pursing of the lips almost drove his niece to open laughter, till she took refuge in gazing about the apartment, which was full of things quaint and curious, — at least to Penelope's unaccustomed eyes. An easel stood in one corner beside the window, with a palette still wet hanging upon its peg, and a stiff stool near by, as though the artist had but just pushed it away. A massive chest of black oak leaned its lid against the wall, which gave support to the rickety cover, and formed a background for a drawing in black and white. Above it, covering almost the side of the room, hung a great Flemish tapestry representing the temptation of Eve, wherein a green serpent was seen curling round a yellow tree to reach a brown apple, while Adam and Eve looked on from behind a hedge of red bushes. Yet so old and mellow were the colors that they blended into a fine, harmonious tone, which matched well with the artist's other belongings; and though the chest beneath it was from France, and the carved table before it from Sweden, and the mantel had been brought hither from an old Italian palace, yet there was no break in the harmony: for fine furnishings are like fine folk, and have power to adapt themselves to their surroundings, and, for the matter of that, the best are at home everywhere.

No whit of all this philosophizing, you may be sure, came into Penelope's mind as she gazed around with wide-open, child-like eyes, her lips parted, and her cheek flushed by the heat from the great logs which blazed at the back of the deep fireplace. She was only vaguely conscious of pleasure in all this warmth and color and beauty. At length Mr. Pepys shut his book, looked at the clock, and vowed they must be going unless the artist came soon, though he would like to have Penelope catch sight of his portraits, for some counted them the best in England.

They had been sitting but a few moments longer when Kneller came in after the brisk fashion which was his wont; but catching sight of Penelope he fell back a step, as if in amazement, and scarcely waiting to say "Good day," he exclaimed to her uncle, "I do entreat your permission to make a sketch of this young lady, whoever she be."

"Ah," answered Mr. Pepys, with a low bow, "such a request from Godfrey Kneller is a compliment indeed, and some day, when my niece is in her best attire, we shall both be only too happy to grant the sitting."

"My good sir," interrupted Kneller, impatiently,

"I would have you know I am an artist, not a *tailor*." When he had got thus far he stopped and bit his lip, and Penelope saw that he had of a sudden remembered that Mr. Pepys's father was of that calling, for he hurried on: "Your niece is of so rare and delicate a beauty that dress is an impertinence which doth rather detract from it than enhance it. Of a truth, I am weary of painting bedizened dames with powder and paint, and patches set on in fantastical shapes of birds and beasts and even coach and four. This simplicity will have all the charms of art blended with nature, and novelty to crown all. I will have her just as she is, with the sunlight falling through the lattice upon that wonderful hair.

"'Tis a strange, mixed type of beauty," he continued, as if talking to himself of some portrait. "The pink and white of the skin are pure English, but the hot red tones in the hair bespeak a more Southern race. That long Spanish eye should go with calm, voluptuous features, and looketh strangely at variance with the petulant nostril and short-lipped, decided mouth beneath it. 'Tis a face full of contradictions, but only the more charming for that; and nothing could be finer to an artist's eye than the flesh tints seen through the bluish shadows of the lawn folds. Yet pardon me if I draw it back a trifle — thus — that the turn of the throat and the curve of the chin be the better seen. So — that is perfect. Prithee, young lady, stir not, but stay exactly as you are while I fetch my canvas."

With this he ran out of the room, and presently returned with a roll of canvas which he fastened to a stretcher and set upon an easel before Penelope. About the floor stood various portraits, so faithful to life that the young visitor, who knew little of the painter's art, almost expected to see them speak. In particular the portrait of the Queen — rather pretty, with soft eyes and a white neck, on which her hair fell in stiff little curls like the tendrils of the grapevines in spring — greatly took her fancy.

"There," said Kneller at last, stepping back that he might view his sketch the better, "'t is little more than a hint, but I can now work it out alone, and perchance Mistress Payne will grant me another sitting on the morrow."

"The working of this great artist," wrote Penelope afterward in her diary, "is surely like ye waving of a magician's wand; for ere I had time to tire of looking about, he had set on his canvas a picture which I should have said was alive, only far, far too butifull for me. I should scarce have known it but for that homesick look in its eyes, and yᵉ string of pearls about yᵉ throat."[1]

[1] Visitors to the National Gallery may have noticed a portrait closely resembling this description. It is labelled in the catalogue, "Portrait of a lady,— unknown,— by Sir Godfrey Kneller." But if the visitor inspect the canvas closely, he will find in the lower left-hand corner, traced in red, the word " Penelope."

CHAPTER XVI.

PENELOPE GOES TO COURT.

> She sails by that rock, the Court,
> Where oft Virtue splits her mast
> And retiredness thinks the port
> Where her fame may anchor cast —
>   Virtue cannot safely sit
>   Where vice is enthroned for wit.

"I AM to go to Court, and 't is come about in the strangest fashion. One would scarce credit it an it were set forth in a play. Folk would say, 'Why doth ye playwright trifle with us thus, and think to trick us into a belief in so unlikely a happening?' Yet all this hath verily come to pass, and in real life too."

Yes, it was indeed, as Penelope wrote in her journal, a strange happening. Just when she and her uncle were worn out with waiting for news from the Duke of Buckingham, and when Mr. Pepys was actually writing to beg the intervention of the Duke of York with the King, his brother, in burst Godfrey Kneller one morning, bubbling over with joy and well-nigh breathless with excitement.

He had been at Whitehall, so his story ran, for a sitting of Queen Catherine, — the last before the finishing of her portrait, — and having with him the sketch of Penelope, had shown it to the Queen as a fancy piece, to be called "Spring;" and she, being mightily taken therewith, had called His Majesty, and bade him say if ever he had seen a face so fair at once and so sad. "'T is 'Spring' indeed," quoth she, "and a very pretty conceit, with the sun on the hair and the dew in the eyes and April in the showery smiling o' the lips."

But His Majesty took the picture to the window, and, after studying it close, looked up and said to the artist, while he twirled his mustachios: —

"Kneller, this is no fancy piece. 'T is a portrait, and a close study at that. This eye, with its tiny mole on the under lid, hath the very trick of life in 't, and that ripple of red brown hair was never imagined save by him who had seen it. Out with it, man, — what name bears thy 'Spring' when she steps forth from this canvas?"

"Thus commanded by royalty," said the painter, "I dared not dissemble, but told him straight 't was the niece of Samuel Pepys, — one Mistress Penelope Payne, but lately come to London from the colony of Virginia."

"'Pepys?' quoth the King; 'Pepys of the Navy Office I trow. He hath besieged me with letters of late, since he hath been in disgrace, begging to come kiss my hand. Well, perchance his banishment hath lasted long enough, — how say you, Kate, shall we have this Mistress Spring and her uncle to our mask next week?'

"The Queen, who, methought, was but too happy at hearing herself thus kindly spoke to by His Majesty, smiled right graciously, and declared she would give much to see the beautiful young stranger; whereupon the Chamberlain, in my hearing, was bidden to despatch a card. Methinks," Kneller added, "it had been no more than civil had he included the artist as well as the subject; but we painters rarely get our deserts, and I bear no malice, and shall feel more than repaid if I catch a glimpse of Mistress Payne in her Court attire."

The good Kneller little knew what service he had done his sitter. He thought he was giving a young girl from the wilderness a taste of Court pleasures. In fact, he was giving her a chance for life. Thus it came to pass that on a February morning a great card arrived at the door of the small house in Seething Lane,— a card with gilt lettering, bidding Mr. Pepys and his niece to a mask at Whitehall a week from that night. Penelope wavered between the heights of hope and the depths of despair; but her uncle was all delight, and talked of costumes till his niece was nearly distracted. She strove to gain his permission to go as a nun, in a black domino; but he would hear no such word.

"If you would catch the King's ear," said Master Worldly-Wise-Man, "ye must first catch his eye." So he talked now of a shepherdess, that the turn of the foot might show to advantage; then of Diana with a bow and arrows, leaving the arm bare; then of the part of St. Cecilia, which, as he said, need cost but little, as his cousin Roger would lend the harp, only that would prevent moving about, and Penelope's walk was the most seizing thing about her.

At last, wearied out, poor Penelope cried: "If in very truth I must trick out a sad heart in such like mumeries, I will go as *Virginia*."

"Ay, and so thou shalt," answered her uncle. "'T is an extraordinary good idea and do please me mightily. For myself, I will be a Spanish cardinal, for I love a scarlet robe, and considering the silver cup I have promised to the clothworkers, methinks I should get the making on't for nothing." And so the matter was settled.

It was scarcely two o'clock on the afternoon of the ball when Betty and Dolly came to Penelope's chamber bearing the dress which her uncle had provided. It was indeed a marvel of ingenuity, and did credit to his taste and imagination. The petticoat was of white satin, wrought richly about the edge with a design of tobacco leaves worked in golden thread. The bodice was finished with a fall of soft yellow lace, and the girdle fell to meet the hem in tassels like the tassels of the Indian corn. About her neck Penelope wore her mother's string of pearls; and on her head they set a crown made in the form of five golden bands, one above the other, and on the upper was writ in brilliants, —

"*Virginia adds a fifth crown.*"

When Penelope looked into her bit of mirror, her heart gave a sudden leap, in spite of all her trouble, at the loveliness which smiled back at her, though she could scarcely connect that radiant vision in any fashion with herself; but when she went downstairs she read in her uncle's eyes a repetition of the flattering story her glass had told her above. It was indeed a tribute that none could fail to pay who saw her as she was that night, — beautiful, exceedingly, with a loveliness far above and beyond that of mere sense; a flame blazing out through her great dark eyes, and burning on her red lips, and breathing from her heaving bosom. She was indeed the soul of love incarnate.

"Child!" cried Master Pepys, "thy cause is as good as won. If the King set eyes on thee as thou art now, he can refuse thee naught. Prithee, Pen, what think ye of *my* looks?"

With this, the tailor in him much delighted with his trappings, he strutted thrice up and down the room in his red cap and gown, with the church lace in front hanging clear to his knees, and with such a solemn air as gave his niece great trouble to keep a grave face. In the midst of his showing off his finery, Betty came running up to say that it was past seven, and the chairs were at the door.

When they were seated, Penelope's crown stood so high that the bearers could scarcely shut down the cover, and they were so long about the business that Mr. Pepys swore roundly at them, and charged them with delaying that they might ask the more pay for their time; but one of the bearers answered that for his part he thought himself well paid by the sight of so beautiful a lady, which Penelope thought wondrous civil for a chair man.

Dolly felt herself a fine lady in a chair of her own. The link boys went before and behind; yet so bad were the streets that, despite their lights, the bearer of Penelope's chair stumbled twice, and the jerk went nigh to throw poor *Virginia* into the mud, and so shook her crown that she feared it could never be set straight, and she fell to crying secretly, which was very weak and foolish.

At the last, when they were come within sight of the palace, her heart quite failed her, and she would have gone back; but she knew her uncle would not hear of it: and I would rather believe that she herself would not in the end have shown herself such a coward. Up the marble steps they went, and, having shown their card, Penelope entered into the disrobing room, and there, after what seemed an eternity, her uncle came for her, and together they passed down the corridor and entered the great ball-room, where was much twanging of fiddles, and tightening of strings, and rosining of bows.

The room was so large that, though many were gathered, they seemed scarcely a handful therein; and as they walked about, so highly polished was the floor, they seemed like two companies walking with their feet together. A subdued buzz of talk was going round, with much laughter and merry-making; but as they entered, Mr. Pepys and his niece, with turbaned Dolly holding up the young lady's train, the talk died away, and but for the protection of her mask Penelope thought she would have died of fright.

In truth the sight itself might well have frightened a maid, for here was such a crew as never gathered save round the lady in "Comus." Satyrs with goat-skin legs jostled devils with horns and hoofs and wicked eyes gleaming through their red masks. Nymphs there were in plenty, and rustic maids, whose bare necks and arms put Penelope to the blush, and made her wonder if the ladies of the Court fancied that country people went thus half-clad. It made Penelope smile, though her heart was in her throat, to fancy such costumes at Middle Plantation.

After the hush which had greeted her entrance, the talk began again, livelier than ever, and Penelope caught some comments which she felt sure concerned herself.

"Who is she?"

"I know not, but know I will ere the evening ends."

"Be not too bold. By the carriage of her head, I could swear she is meet company for thy betters."

"Look at that strange blackamoor who bears

her train. Is she really black, or a maid of honor, disguised like the Jennings and her mischievous friend, when they scandalized the Court by playing at orange girl before the theatre doors?"

So vext and wrought up, half with wrath and half with terror, was Penelope at all this bold talk, that she would even now have run away; but it was too late. A blare of trumpets and a crash of all the instruments together announced the coming of the King's party, and the Lord Chamberlain with a wave of his white wand crowded every one back against either wall to make room for the royal entry.

Oh, how Penelope's heart beat as she turned her eyes to the door! In they came. First the King and Queen, together and unmasked; then a bevy of ladies, who, as it seemed to the little provincial maiden, must wear their masks to hide their shame at the bareness of their bosoms; and after them, again, a crowd of gallants in every sort of fantastic costume.

As the King and Queen passed close before Penelope she had opportunity to study them both. The Queen was short and dumpy of figure, but full of a comely graciousness which lent beauty to a face otherwise ill-favored, with large protruding teeth which pushed out her lips like a negro's. The King, Penelope thought, with his tall figure and rich dress, was all a king should be, though the deep furrows of brow and cheek belied his title of "The Merry Monarch." Even to Penelope's untutored eye that saturnine face spoke a melancholy which strove in vain to find mirth in excess.

Their Majesties moved slowly down the hall, pausing now to note and smile at some costume stranger, if possible, than the rest, where all were strange; now to comment on some extraordinarily rich and striking dress. When they had reached the head of the room, His Majesty with great courtliness handed the Queen to her seat upon a gilded chair covered in velvet with an embroidered canopy above it; but instead of taking the chair which stood beside it, he returned to the other end of the room, and summoned to his side one who played the rôle of soothsayer,—a tall figure in Oriental garb, with long white beard, and flowing robes over which hung chains and rich jewelry, which, had they been real, must have exhausted the treasure-houses of the East.

"Come, good Master Soothsayer!" cried the King, "draw near and I will have you test your powers. We will have up the ladies of the Court one by one, and I will try if that keen eye of yours can see through a mask, and that wagging beard let slip a true prophecy."

At these words, all who could decently leave the Queen circled close about the group at the lower end of the hall, and one after another the ladies drew near; and by the peals of laughter which followed the soothsayer's words Penelope judged that they must have struck home. Absorbed in looking and listening as she was, she had wholly forgotten herself, when of a sudden, to her infinite alarm, the usher of the white rod plucked her softly by the sleeve, saying: "Lady, the soothsayer wishes to tell your fortune, and the King bids you come forward."

Poor Penelope shrank back in terror very unsuited to her part, and would have begged to be excused; but her uncle frowned upon her, which frightened her more than aught else, and at the same time his arm seized and fairly pushed her forward, till she found herself the centre of the brilliant, laughing circle which had gathered about the King and the sorcerer.

Here Penelope's natural grace and courtesy untaught of courts came to her aid, and made her a fit centre for even such a circle. Kneeling, as she had observed the rest do, she bent her head and kissed the King's hand, and then, rising, bowed after a more stately fashion to the soothsayer.

"Are you prepared, young woman, to listen to

your fate?" asked the sham sorcerer, with a solemnity which would have befitted the cardinal saying mass at St. Peter's."

"Let it be a kind one," murmured Penelope with fast-beating heart.

"Hearken, then; I say it, and even as I say it so shall it be. Ye shall have many strange experiences; but all shall end well,— at least for yourself. Honor and fortune await you, if you have the wit and the courage to grasp them. It is your destiny to live to a good old age here in England, loaded with riches, and never more to return to that wilderness whence you came hither and where all the land is divided twixt savages and rebels."

What with amazement that the soothsayer had guessed so much of her history, and a superstitious feeling which she could not shake off that there was something of omen in the words, Penelope was quite overcome. She gave a great gasp, swayed to and fro, and would have fallen but for the outstretched hand of the King, which caught her.

"Enough of this folly," cried His Majesty's voice. "Chamberlain, bid every one unmask!"

The diversion which these words made gave Penelope time to recover herself, so that when she too withdrew her mask, her color and her self-command had both come back. But when on looking up she recognized in the unmasked soothsayer the man who had stood in her uncle's dining-room only a fortnight since, she was nearly overcome once more.

"Your Majesty," said Buckingham, returning Penelope's gaze of surprise with a look of amusement, "here is the young Virginia damsel for whom I craved a card to your mask to-night."

"By Heaven! and 't is the original of Kneller's 'Spring' also. Those bright eyes have won two knights at once. Well done, Villiers!" cried the King, who seemed to Penelope quite transformed by the smile which lighted up his face, "ye had always good taste in women, — far better, to our thinking, than in men."

At this Buckingham looked suddenly abashed, though Penelope knew not why.

"Young lady," continued the King, graciously turning to Penelope, "be ye 'Spring' or 'Virginia,' or some fair unknown visitor from our provinces over sea, ye are welcome to your mother country! And is your father with you?"

"Nay, Your Majesty," answered Penelope, hardly able from fright to utter a word "my mother was too ill to permit his leaving her."

"Ah, then, 't is your brother perchance who hath been your guardian?"

"Alas, Your Majesty," answered Penelope, "I have no brother."

"Neither father nor brother!" exclaimed the King. "It must be pressing business indeed that brings a young maid three thousand miles alone. To whose charge prithee did you come, for I suppose ye dwell not alone in London?"

"I am come to the care of mine uncle, who is come hither with me to-night, and who stands near the wall yonder."

"Ah, yes, yes, I do recall now," began His Majesty, when a lady who stood near him, very handsome, but bold of eye and bare of bosom, said, addressing Penelope with scant courtesy of tone or manner, "How dare ye come across the ocean, and to the very door of the Court, with no better guardian?"

"Pray, Madam," answered Penelope, lifting her clear eyes full upon the speaker, "what harm could befall me at Court? Is not the *King* here?"

Penelope was at a loss to comprehend the effect of her words; but she feared there was something sadly out of the way in them, for she saw the ladies hide their faces behind their fans, and the gentlemen bite their mustachios and stare hard at the toes of their boots, while the Duke of Buckingham shook with laughter, and whispered to his next neighbor, "The Duchess hath caught it fair from the little savage, — she 'd best not meddle with her again. Besides, my Lady hath need to mark her words carefully, for she can no longer take such liberties with the King as when she was the Countess of Castlemaine."

Only His Majesty kept the gravity of his face unmoved, and replied still more kindly to Penelope, "Ay, ye have said aright, — the King is here and ye have naught to fear. Now gentlemen," he added turning to those around, "choose your partners for the brantle. Buckingham, bid the musicians strike a tune!"

With this there was much moving to and fro. Very noble the procession was, and a great pleasure to see; but there were two in that hall who gave it little heed, those left thus for an instant alone together, — the man who ruled it all, and the little rustic who looked on it for the first time: yet somehow Penelope feared the King least of all.

"Tell me," he said in a voice which of itself gave her courage, so kind was it, "is it some sorrow that hath driven you thus over seas, my child? Your face is too sad for one so young, and surely you have ne'er made such a journey without grave occasion."

"The time and place, Your Majesty," answered

Penelope, "scarce befit my sad story, else would I crave the boon of laying it before you."

The maid choked and could say no more. "You say truly," said the King, "that this is neither the time nor the place; but we will set a time and find a place for the hearing. Mr. Pepys," he added, turning to that gentleman, who courtier like stood just near enough to catch what was going forward without appearing to hear, "ye have twice written asking permission to come kiss our hand. Your petition is granted; we will arrange an audience both for you and your niece. Let it be to-morrow — stay — to-morrow is mortgaged to the ambassadors of Spain and Sweden. We will say Friday — no, Friday is unlucky; and on Saturday I go a-hunting at Windsor. Well, ye shall hear of the time later"

Pepys would fain have burst out with a florid speech of gratitude, but the King cut him short and bade him make ready to take his niece in to supper, whither he shortly led the way with a lady whose beauty was so dazzling that it fairly took away Penelope's breath. She was dressed as Britannia, with a burnished helmet from which rose a great cluster of white ostrich plumes, whose whiteness could not surpass the brow beneath, or the neck, bare save for the shower of raven-black curls which fell over it. Her breast-plate was of beaten gold, with a group of pearls in the centre worth a man's ransom, and her mantle was caught at the shoulder with a brooch of rubies, and the sheer lawn of the sleeve was bound above the elbow with a band of gems which flashed in Penelope's eyes as the radiant vision passed.

"Who is she? O uncle, who is she, — that lovely lady, queenlier than the queen, whose beauty strikes me breathless?"

"Ay, mark her," quoth Pepys, as he carefully gathered his robe over his arm and prepared to follow the procession. "Ye'll ne'er see anything to match her. Did ever ye set eyes on such an excellent *taille* or such a complexion (all her own too); and then that sweet eye and little Roman nose, — oh, there is none like *La Belle* Stuart in the whole of England! And yet, child, I heard three gentlemen say that you were the fairer of the two, and that there was none could match you for grace and stateliness."

As the procession moved into the Banqueting Hall with much mirth and laughter, Penelope fell to wondering how the son of the martyred king could find heart to make merry on the spot where his father had suffered, — ay, and gone forth to his death through that very window now hung gayly with lanterns. As she gazed around upon the panels blazoned with heraldry, and upon the great oaken beams which supported the open-timbered roof, her mind was carried strangely back to the rude rafters and bare boards of the rough Court House at Middle Plantation. Yes, she could see once more the grim faces of the fierce old Governor and his counsellors; and the crowd of figures that thronged around her as she sat on that Court House bench seemed far more substantial than the liveried lackeys who stood before her now, waiting to bring her portions of the pheasants which lay in state on their platters of gold, or of the great peacock, which, with his tail outspread, decorated one end of the long board beneath the twinkling candles.

Penelope raised her hand to her brow as if to brush away the fog which clung around her mind. "Which," she wondered, "is the true Penelope,— the maiden in the prisoner's dock, hand clasping hand with a convicted felon, or this princess with golden crown and sweeping draperies at the King's levee?" A conviction flashed upon her, as it does on all of us at certain crises, that she was but a puppet, made to dance and laugh and sing, or to kneel and weep and pray, according as the hand behind the scenes pulled the strings. Thus she sat silent and cast down, and could touch no morsel of the feast spread before her; but her uncle had no such sentimental scruples.

"'T is a fine supper," quoth he, "a prodigious fine supper; but the venison pasty is very palpable beef, which is not handsome."

CHAPTER XVII.

A PRIVATE INTERVIEW

" Full little knowest thou that hast not tried
What Hell it is in sueing long to bide,
To lose good dayes that might be better spent,
To wast long nights in pensive discontent,
To speed to-day, to be put back to-morrow,
To feed on hope, to pine with feare and sorrow."

ON the day after the ball Penelope spent half her time hanging out of the little latticed window, waiting and watching for a messenger who never came. The next day it was as bad, and her heart began to lose its courage, and her cheek to lose its color, till at length her uncle chid her, but gently, saying: "'T is little ye know of Courts, child, else would ye not expect the King to be a man of business, who keeps his appointments clerk-like."

"But, Uncle, he did promise."

"Oh, he did promise," echoed her uncle, jestingly. "I would have you know, Penelope, that there be men in London Tower with a promise of fat office in their pocket, and men swinging from the gibbet who died with promises ringing in their ears."

"Then," cried Penelope, flying out in a passion, "I say an unkept promise is no better than a lie, and a lie is most unkingly."

"Hush, hush, girl!" whispered Pepys, hastily, glancing at the door to make sure that no one had overheard the bold words. "The King is the King, and little good comes of speaking evil of those in authority. Have patience, and time will pass the quicker."

"Have patience!" cried Penelope, mockingly, and with anger in her voice. "Oh, I am sick of the sound of the word. 'Tis easy to say 'have patience,' but when the horologe is ticking away a man's life 'tis a mean virtue, and little to be commended save to time-servers."

It may be that the last word hit Mr. Pepys a little hard, for he flounced about in his chair, quite forgetful of his dignity, and turned his back upon Penelope, while she in turn sat tapping the floor with the heel of her little slipper, when in came Betty very opportunely, bearing biscuit and wine, and on the tray beside them, a letter. Yes, a letter from the King's secretary appointing an interview for the morrow morning at eleven o'-clock.

A Private Interview.

The summons set Mr. Pepys in good humor once more, and Penelope, ashamed of her peevishness, ran to him and caught him about the neck and begged him to forgive her; and so they were friends once more.

The next day came at last, though to one little maid in London it seemed that all the clocks had hands of lead, and that the very sun stood still on the dial plates.

"This morning being Thursday," says Penelope's journal, "we betook ourselves once more to the palace at Whitehall. 'T were idle to set down my feelings; they were past describing, almost past realizing. I knew naught save that ye supreme hour of my life was come, and yet I was tying my hood and smoothing my bands even as I had done hundreds of times before, and instead of finding all things blurred, my senses did but seem so sharpened that they took note of even the least thing. My uncle chid me for uneasiness and haste to be gone, but though to me he seemed slower than the creeping of the muddy Thames, we did at length set out, and when we were come to ye palace it wanted yet a half hour of the time ye King had set; wherfore to while away ye uneasiness of waiting, mine uncle drew me into the privy garden, where we did walk up and down, sheltered from the wind and comfortable enough in body, but I at least much shaken in sole by an aggony of fear and anxiety."

This garden wherein poor Penelope walked up and down so shaken in "sole" was the pride of all London, and especially of Mr. Pepys, who, for all he plumed himself so much upon his knowledge of human nature, fancied now that he could divert his niece from her sorrow by pointing out the windows of the different maids of honor and the extraordinary fine lace on the underclothing marked B V. with a coronet above, which hung upon the lines beneath the windows of the Duchess of Cleveland. Penelope looked and nodded and smiled a sad little absent smile, more pathetic than a flood of tears.

Another turn in this walk brought them to a sun dial of stone richly carved with vines and strange intertwining dragons. It had been in its prime a thing of quaint and curious beauty, but unluckily, in spite of being surrounded with the protection of an iron railing, it had been broken by a drunken gallant in some midnight brawl, and now was so sunken and out of shape that its hand no longer truly marked the hour. Beneath its shattered face some wag, who knew well the foibles of Charles's Court, had written: —

A Private Interview.

> "This place for a dial was too insecure,
> Since a guard and a garden could not it defend;
> For so near the Court they could never endure
> Any witness to show how their time they misspend."

As though to show that not all those at Court deserved such harsh satire, the little door at one end of the garden opened even while Penelope and her uncle bent over the dial, and a short and straggling procession crossed the garden. First came two priests, their cowls covering their heads, and the foremost one bearing a crucifix of silver and ebony. They were followed by six little boys in black petticoats, and what looked to Penelope like white nightgowns over, each carrying a lighted taper. Then walking alone came the Queen, a long veil covering her from head to foot, and giving to her short figure a dignity which it lacked in gayer dress. Finally a knot of Court ladies in sober attire hurried after, and then the little gate closed again with another clang.

Penelope had half a mind as the procession passed to throw herself at the Queen's feet and entreat her protection and intercession. Indeed she did take a step forward; but her uncle, perceiving her intention, whispered, "Are ye mad? The Queen's favor is the last road to the King's. Keep back, I say!"

Penelope wavered, and then stopped and drew her veil closer.

"The Court is divided 't wixt mass and mumming," said Mr. Pepys, as the gate closed; but his niece noted that he crossed himself as the priest passed, and she wondered if there were any ground for the charge of popery which she had heard that some brought against him.

The shadow on the dial crept on, till at length, after a time that seemed well-nigh endless, an usher, very gorgeously attired, approached, and bade them follow him to the King's presence-chamber. Through the grilled gateway they passed, and down the long stone gallery, which echoed to the sound of their footsteps, till at last their guide paused before a door richly hung with velvet of a deep purple color. This curtain being softly drawn aside from within, they passed through, and found themselves in the royal ante-chamber. A clerk seated at a table, busily employed in sorting papers, looked up at their entrance, and bade Mr. Pepys be seated, as the King would receive the young lady first, and alone. Penelope, looking at her uncle, saw his face cloud, but whether with anxiety on her behalf, or vexation that his own suit should thus be put off, she knew not.

For herself, robbed thus of the support of his

presence, she felt ready to sink to the earth. Her knees trembled so, she must needs grasp the folds of the curtain which hung between the presence-chamber and the ante-room. But the usher led her forward, over soft Eastern carpets, between the great porphyry jars which stood on either side of the doorway, to the table where the King sat. Kneeling down, Penelope kissed his hand in silence, scarcely able to command herself enough to utter a word. The King, as if comprehending the disorder of her mind, raised her gently, and setting her in the deep-cushioned velvet chair opposite his own, bade the lackey bring her a glass of wine, that therein she might find strength and refreshment. He watched her in silence, while her trembling fingers broke the biscuit and held the goblet to her lips; then, greatly to her relief, he was graciously pleased himself to begin the conversation, toying as he spoke with the drooping ears of a tiny coal-black spaniel which lay on the table beside him, its tail playing sad havoc with the state papers which were scattered in heaps about him.

"So," began the King, smiling, "you are come all the way from Virginia. I trust you are not a little rebel against the authority of your sovereign,— not of those who, as I hear, have earned the inglorious title of 'White Aprons' by having on one occasion taken shelter behind the petticoats of women." With this the King burst out laughing, and Penelope blushed furiously as she remembered how she herself had been the first to cast the aspersion.

"Nay, Your Majesty," she answered, "my father served in Berkeley's army, and the Governor had no stancher supporter in the colony."

"And what say they across the water of Berkeley?"

"I trust I speak not too much in bitterness," answered Penelope, "when I say they do call him a hard man, tyrannical to those under him, and passing cruel to a fallen foe."

"By the Lord, maiden, I do believe ye speak no more than the truth. A report of my commissioners hath lately reached me which do vex me sorely. They say he hath sacrificed twenty victims since Bacon's death, — twenty! Why, the old fool hath taken more lives in that naked country than I for my father's murder!"

"And these, Your Majesty," urged Penelope, timidly, "were neither murderers, nor even rebels, save against the tyranny of Berkeley."

"Why, how now! I thought ye were of Berkeley's party?"

"We *were*, Your Majesty; but certain things

have of late greatly changed our hearts. My father, who ever inclines to mercy, could still bear to see punishment, but not injustice, and so wrought upon was he by the sentence of one of the poor gentlemen taken after Bacon's death, and doomed to die, but respited till April, that he hath vowed to save him if he could, the more that he owed him thanks for the saving of his life at a battle near Jamestown, when the sword was at his heart. 'T is at my father's command that I am now come over seas to plead in turn for the saving of the life of his preserver. Oh, pardon, I pray you, pardon!" So crying, Penelope fell once more upon her knees, her hand holding out the petition, her eyes upturned in deepest supplication.

As she watched his face her heart sank, and she felt that she must have plead her cause ill indeed; for instead of melting, or showing aught of sympathy, the King only smiled. "Methinks," quoth he, "you have not yet given sufficient reason why you, a maid scarce eighteen summers old, if my eye deceives me not, — and it seldom plays me false in judging the age of women, — why, I say, your father sends you alone and unprotected such a distance upon such an errand. Were this condemned man a lover you could scarce do more than brave such difficulties and dangers in his behalf."

At these words, which showed but too clearly that the King had penetrated the disguise behind which her heart had sought to hide, she answered steadily, through all the red rushing over neck and cheek and brow: "I pray thee, Sire, spare a maiden's confession. I could scarce, e'en had I a ready tongue and full command of myself, make any comprehend the strange chances which did overcome my former enmity. I can but say that whereas I did once hold Bryan Fairfax my deadliest foe, I do now count him most of all the world my friend — my love."

Never in all her life had Penelope looked so beautiful as now, when, wholly forgetful of herself, absorbed in her great love and devotion, she knelt as at an altar, pleading with liquid eyes upturned to her King, as to her God. The eyes which looked down upon her took on all at once a new look, an evil look, — a look neither godly nor kingly.

"Do you indeed care so much for this pardon?" he asked.

"*Care!*" cried Penelope. "Oh that there were any sacrifice I might be thought worthy to make for such a reward!"

"Why then," said the king, "I have a mind to try you."

"Ah!" exclaimed Penelope, "Your Majesty shall see how gratefully I do accept the trial. Ay, though it be a dungeon, I will dwell there in cheerfulness; or a scaffold, I will die thanking and blessing your name."

"Nay, nay," answered the king, "I would scarce care to see so much loveliness shut up in the darkness of London Tower, nor yet untimely cut off on Tyburn Hill. Trust me, the trial whereof I spake was no such killing matter. Come, my pretty one," he cried with a sudden change of voice and manner, "let us two strike a bargain. What say you to a pardon for your lover, and for yourself, — the favor of the King of England?"

Penelope would scarcely have been able to interpret the meaning of these words had they not been accompanied by such an amorous glance as brought back to her her father's words of warning: "Trust not the gentlemen of the Court, — nay, not the King himself, for with all his virtues he holdeth women but lightly."

"Sire," she cried, "I know you do but jest. Could I believe you for one instant spoke in earnest, I would pray you tear the pardon, and I would go home and bid Bryan Fairfax die on the scaffold, as an honest man should, to save the honor of his affianced wife." As she spoke these words in her indignation, she rose to her feet and stood before the King undismayed, no longer a suppliant, but a woman.

The King, sovereign though he was, looked ill at ease, and twisting about in his chair began once more to play with the spaniel. As he showed his face it was as if two spirits therein did contend for the mastery. At last the better prevailed, and shed over his face such a glow of emotion and benignity as made clear to Penelope's mind the love which his subjects bore him.

"Thou hast spoke bravely, — bravely and truly, my child," said he, "and 't was ill done jesting with a love like thine, which will dare and suffer all save loss of honor. Leave me now, — I am weary, — and bid thine uncle come next week. I will look over the petition and will have the secretary make out the pardon, which I will straightway sign, and thou shalt have it with no other condition but that thou do offer up a prayer for thy sovereign in some chapel of thy native wilderness."

"Sire!" cried she, "I will pray God preserve the King, and petition every night and every morning that Heaven continue him in his present happiness."

"Happiness!" said he, his face darkening, — "happiness is a word for children, idiots, and angels. How should a king look to be happy, —

least of all a king badgered by his wife, baited by his ministers, hated by his creatures, ruled by — "

Ere he had uttered the last word, a tapestry in one corner of the presence-chamber swayed a little, then was raised, and beneath it stood the lady of the Court, Barbara Villiers, Baroness of Nonsuch, Countess of Southampton, and Duchess of Cleveland. Her gown was of brocade, set off with a girdle stiff with precious stones, which shone forth with double splendor as she stood against the dark folds of the purple drapery, one white arm, from which the sleeve had fallen, raised, and revealing all its tapering roundness, ere she let it slowly drop to her side.

The King looked upon her, and, as he looked, the old sense of subjection which had held him in this woman's thrall for so many years, from which of late he had flattered himself that he was free, returned with renewed power. She saw it in an instant and was quick to push her advantage.

"It is my hour, Your Majesty," she said, speaking scarce above her breath, but holding him by the spell of her eyes.

The King hesitated a moment, looking first at her, then at the figure opposite, with its severely simple drapery, its pure pale face, its proud eyes, and its halo of red-brown hair.

Once more the angels struggled within him, and this time the baser conquered. A hardness settled down like a mask over his face.

"Yes, Madam," he answered, "it *is* your hour. Mistress Payne, your audience is at an end; you may withdraw."

Penelope noted nothing of the drama enacted thus before her eyes, nor did she know after what fashion she withdrew from the presence-chamber, — if she walked or flew. All she felt sure of was the precious pardon. "Pardon! Pardon!" every wheel in London echoed it. "Pardon! Pardon!" every oar beat time to it in the barges along the Thames. "Pardon! Pardon!" the church bells rang it as they sounded out the hours. Pardon for Bryan Fairfax!

CHAPTER XVIII.

A FOY.

> "A very merry, dancing, drinking,
> Laughing, quaffing, and unthinking
> Time."

"MR. SAMUEL PEPYS, his compliments to Mr. John Dryden and wife, and begs the honor of their company at the Dog Tavern, Southwark, on Monday night, to a Foy given in honour of Mistress Penelope Payne before her setting sail in the 'White Lady' for the Colony of Virginia."

Such pleasure did good Mr. Pepys find in the despatching of this and other like missives, and, indeed, in the whole preparation of this farewell feast, that his niece could not find it in her heart to tell him how little it was to her liking, or how small a zest had an anxious mind for merry-making. But the pardon, duly signed and countersigned, lay on her breast, and that was joy enough in itself. She knew, moreover, that though she spent her nights in tears and prayers, she could not hasten, by one slow minute, the departure of the "White Lady," which was to drop down the Thames on Tuesday morning, and she bethought her that she was in duty bound to be as cheerful as she could in these last hours, if only to requite her uncle for the kindness with which he had taken her and her concerns into his care.

When, therefore, he brought with huge delight all these billets to her, she forced herself to smile, and offer him thanks for the planning of such a festival in her honor. Privately she wondered much that he should hold the feast at a hostelry rather than in his own house; for the Virginians were so wont to look upon their houses as their castles, and to bid both friends and strangers enter at pleasure and make them welcome to all within, that they could conceive no hospitality outside its walls, still less at an "ordinary," which in Virginia was a miserable shanty without even the decencies of life. But Penelope was learning by slow degrees that many things in this wider world were different from the ways of her provincial home.

Among the guests bidden to the feast, much to the maiden's delight, were Captain and Mrs. Bennett. (Ah, how she gave thanks to Heaven that their ship was stayed till now with loading, and that the homeward voyage was not to be undertaken with strangers!) With them were to come Mr. Godfrey Kneller, not yet knighted, and Mr. Dryden, who wrote to say that he should do himself the honor to accept Mr. Pepys's invitation, but that his wife was ill and could not be of the party.

Sooth to say, Penelope sorrowed little over the prospect of her absence; she felt, though she could hardly tell why, that she fared less well with the women than with the men here in this strange new old world. She counted it the result of the quaintness of her dress and the uncouthness of her manners, which, as she said to herself, are more prone to strike the quick eye of women than the duller perceptions of men.

The morning before the foy, it chanced that the Duke of Buckingham called at Seething Lane, ostensibly on navy business; but the real object of his visit transpired ere long, for after repeating much Court gossip anent the appearance of the new beauty, who (so he said) was counted to outshine even the Duchess of Richmond, and to be the first stranger that ever Lady Castlemaine honored with her jealousy, he dropped, quite by accident as it were, the remark that he had heard from Mr. Dryden how a foy was to be held at the Dog Tavern, in

Mistress Payne's honor: but he had told him this could not be, else had he himself surely been of the number of those bidden.

"Nay, nay, my Lord!" answered Mr. Pepys with a fine bow, though looking a trifle taken aback, "I should never have dreamed of taking the liberty to ask your Lordship to so poor a feast as the best 'the Dog's' kitchen can provide."

"Thanks," answered His Grace, cheerfully. "Methinks I am like to go to the dogs without awaiting any bidding of thine, Master Pepys."

After this he turned and bade Penelope farewell very graciously, wishing her a fair wind and a safe return, and that she might find all in Virginia to her liking, congratulating her upon her success, and praying his regards to his cousin by marriage, — Bryan Fairfax.

"Is it too late, my Lord, to beg you to favor us with your company at the feast?" asked Mr. Pepys, with his hand upon his breast.

"I do be much beholden by the invitation," quoth the Duke, laying his hand likewise upon the ruffles over his heart, "and I grieve that it comes too late to be accepted, as I am bound by another engagement; but I pray you at your foy to give one toast from me: 'The Virginia Beauty — to our eyes a meteor — in our hearts a fixed star.'"

With this, feeling perhaps that he had no other speech at hand so pat and pretty, and being enough a courtier to like to retire on a success, he bowed himself from the room, and Penelope ran away to her chamber to finish the packing of her chest. Her heart was much touched to find upon her chest of drawers a little worn pincushion, made of two shells and a bit of damask which she had seen in the housekeeper's room.

"Dear Mrs. Fane," cried she, as she heard the housekeeper's step outside the door, "I cannot take this, for I know what store you do set by it."

"Ay," answered the old woman, the wrinkles of her parched skin puckering still more, till her face looked like the skin of a shrivelled winter apple, "I do in truth set much store by it, for 't was my husband brought me the shells on his last voyage home from the Indies, and the damask was given me by a lady from the clippings of her wedding-gown; but I set more store by thee, and I would have thee keep it to remember a crabbed old woman whose heart hath been strangely soft like to thee." At this, Penelope, whose heart was too full for words, threw her arms about Mrs. Fane's neck and their tears fell together. Oh blessed welding power of love and sympathy!

It was six o'clock when Mr. Pepys and his

niece set out by chair over London Bridge, and her uncle pointed out to Penelope the spot where he was near to breaking his leg one night through falling in a hole where no light was set, and more shame to the watch. "Nay, never shake that pretty head of thine, Penelope; 'twas not the unsteadiness of my legs that did bewray me, for though I had in truth passed the evening at a supper, 'twas gave by a man too mean to provide enough liquor to make his guests drunk withal."

"Indeed, dear Uncle, I thought no such thing," said Penelope, who in truth had come to the habit of smiling and nodding her head and even saying "yea" and "nay" by rote and quite at random; which ordinarily mattered little, for to Master Pepys the sound of his own voice was so sweet a music that it quite shut out the sound of another's, and a listener was but a target to be hit or missed by his discourse.

The great fire had destroyed so many houses that there were some desolate places to be passed, and Penelope's heart was in her mouth for fear of footpads and highwaymen. Glad was she as they passed up High Street and neared Kent Road, when the cheerful lantern of the Dog Tavern gleamed full in sight, and the fresh painted sign with its couchant dog, which had taken the place of the old tabard, told them that they had arrived at the famous hostelry. Though the new front, raised since the fire, detracted somewhat from its ancient look, yet it was the same old Tabard Inn at which the Canterbury pilgrims had gathered, and it was in the Pilgrims' Room that the table was set, and on the gallery over it hung a faded picture of that other feast held here by the pilgrims before their setting forth. Though the room was private, the door stood open into the main hall, where there was much coming and going of men and maids.

Presently in came Mr. Dryden, very gay, in a purple velvet coat and flowered waistcoat; Mr. Godfrey Kneller, still finer, in a vest of white satin, the King's artist medal on his breast, and over his shoulder a short cavalier cloak of crimson velvet, lined also with white satin and tied with silken tassels, very handsome.

"Faith," whispered Pepys, "it vexes me that I did wear this sad-colored suit when the rest be so fine."

"Heed it not, dear Uncle," said Penelope, jestingly; "they may count thee in half-mourning for the loss of thy niece."

"'T is true. Thou sayest well," he answered, taking all quite gravely.

At this point in bustled Captain Bennett and his spouse, — he in rough suit of Frisian cloth, plain and blunt, like the bluff sailor he was; but his wife with a hint of finery in her apparel, and a somewhat mincing gait, which must not be set down to her discredit, for many a woman changes her walk to suit her company.

"Ah, my child," she exclaimed, kissing Penelope on both cheeks, "it was like thee not to forget thine old friends for all thy fine new ones. In sooth, I see thee still just thy simple self."

"Indeed, Mrs. Bennett, if I am still myself 't is no credit to me, but only that I know not how to be any one else; and of a truth, the more I see of this strange new world the more I cling to old friends, tried and true, like you and the captain, — and when I think of resting my eyes once more on the blue line of the Virginia shore, and sailing in between the two capes and through the broad bay, and up the yellow James to the little wharf—"

As she reached these words the girl's voice faltered suddenly and broke; and her eyes, which had been set in a wide, far-seeing gaze, like a mystic in a trance, suddenly ceased from their vision, as if the future were too joyful or too dreadful to look upon, and the tears welled up in their brown depths, and stood for a moment like

A Foy.

a diamond fringe on the curling length of her eyelashes; but at the instant Mr. Pepys came to them and made his best bow to Mrs. Bennett, who answered it with a courtesy she had learned of a lady's maid, who had caught it from a duchess. And so, all being ready, the party sat down, — Penelope at the head of the table next her uncle, Mr. Dryden next her, and Mrs. Bennett next her uncle Pepys, then Godfrey Kneller and Captain Bennett on either side; but the great oaken table was so long the party only half filled it, and the candles being all set at one end, Penelope could fancy that end which was half hidden in darkness to be filled with shadowy pilgrims with the poet at their head. She spoke her thoughts to her next neighbor.

"Ay, of a truth," answered Mr. Dryden, "I can see them all, — their humors, their features, and their very dress, as distinctly as if they supped with us here at the Tabard to-night."

None took up his words; for all save Penelope were giving more heed to the table than to the talk. The first dish that was set on was of marrow bones, and this was followed by three pullets and a neat's tongue, with two dozen larks, all in a dish; and when it seemed as though none could eat more, the maid came again from the kitchen bearing a flaming pudding alight with brandy. To wash all down withal, there were both Fayal and Canary, which, for her part, Penelope scarcely tasted; but the gentlemen swallowed such mighty draughts thereof as shortly loosened their tongues so that all went merrily enough. Mr. Pepys, who had brought his violin, now stood up; and after much pecking at the strings as I have seen a woodpecker tap at the bark of a tree, he tucked it under his chin, and drawing his bow, set it first to jigging merrily and then to sobbing plaintively (for of a truth he was a rare musician), till Penelope found it hard to keep back the too ready tears.

Next, he would have Penelope sing "*Gaze not on Swans*," and after that "*Beauty Retire*," and then "*Love will find out the Way*," which she did not like, for the place seemed to her too public, and the more so, that while she was singing there came into the room two strangers having on masks and long dominos, — one black, one purple, — which covered them close from head to foot, so there was no recognizing them. She was frightened, and would have stopped short; but her uncle whispered to her to take no notice, for that it was naught out of the common for gentlemen to wander about thus unknown, to pick up whatever of fun and merriment might be going at the various taverns of the town.

So she went on, though somewhat falteringly, for seeing these muffled forms standing there in the doorway. But her heart was in the words, and found its way to her voice, moving her hearers as only the soul behind the voice can do for all the art in the world.

> "You may train the eagle
>   To stoop to your fist
> Or you may inveigle
>   The phœnix o' the East —
> The lioness ye may move her
>   To give o'er her prey;
> But you 'll ne'er stop a lover —
>   He'll find out the way."

What was her surprise, as she sang, to hear the tinkling notes of some strange instrument, and to see one of the masked visitors leaning against the frame of the doorway draw from under his cloak a mandolin and touch the strings thereof to so sweet a harmony with the voice of the singer as drew forth a great clapping of hands from the company when the two had finished.

"Come in, gentlemen, whoever you be," cried Mr. Pepys. "I love you already for your music's sake, and a good tune doth richly merit a good supper. Sit ye down, therefore, and I will order plates set for you."

"We thank you, worthy master, and we do accept the invitation as heartily as 't is offered withal." So spoke the companion of the mandolin player, and straightway both took chairs opposite Penelope and sat them down.

When they were seated, Mr. Pepys toasted the "White Lady" and her gallant Captain, to which all drank with a right good will. Captain Bennett rose in his place, his cheek red with honest blushes and his nose with honest Canary. "Damme!" he cried, striving to swear away his embarrassment. "I have no skill to make speeches; but by the Lord, I thank ye all, and if ever any one of you is minded to make a voyage on the 'White Lady,' there's a berth at your service, — yes, damme, there is." Thumping another emphasis with his fist, the Captain sat down, greeted by another round of cheers, and much clinking of goblets set down noisily on the board.

When they had finished, Mr. Dryden arose with much ceremony, and bowing like a mandarin to each of the company in turn, he drew from his pocket, and asked permission to read aloud, a neat copy of verses addressed to Penelope, — stanzas wherein she was committed to the care of the ocean nymphs, and they were warned that they must play no tricks with so precious a freight, nor let loose wind or wave till she was set in safety on her native shore.

"Call ye this stuff poetry?" whispered one of the masks to his comrade. "I have a fellow in my service could reel you off better by the yard."

Penelope marvelled much at the stranger's incivility, and felt mightily tempted to let him know who it was whom he was criticising with such ignorant freedom. Mr. Pepys too, whose ear appeared to grow the sharper as his eye grew dull, must have caught the whispered words, for he turned to the new-comer, and said with a tone of ill-suppressed irony, —

"Perchance, Sir Mask, you who seem so good a judge of poetry will give us some verses in honor of Mistress Penelope Payne, the young lady for whom we hold the foy to-night."

"Why, so I will, with pleasure," answers the Mask, as bold as brass, "an ye will give me permission to sing it; for I have oft heard lines go well enough to the accompaniment of the lute which had sounded monstrous flat without."

With this he rose, and drawing his cloak close about his wrist as one who fears his dress may betray him, he began : —

"What a dull fool was I
  To think so gross a lie
  As that I ever was in love before.
  I have perhaps known one or two
  With whom I was content to be
  At that which they call keeping company.
  But after all that they could do
  I still could be with none;
  Their absence never made me shed a tear,
  And I can truly swear
  That, till my eyes first gazed on you,
  I ne'er beheld the thing I could adore."

So soft was the tone of the singer's voice and so intent the gaze he bent upon Penelope that she hung her head and knew not where to look; but the others all clapped hands, and with one voice (save for Mr. Dryden) cried, "Go on!" The stranger, so urged, continued: —

"She that would raise a noble love must find
  Ways to beget a passion for her mind:
  She must be that which she to be would seem,
  For all true love is founded on esteem.
  She must be — what said I? — she must be *you*,
  None but yourself that miracle can do."

Then he made an end, and waving Penelope a mighty fine salute, he sat down.

"Bravo!" cried Kneller. "'T is as pretty a love-song as ever I heard."

"Sir, whoever you be," quoth Mr. Pepys, "you do my niece honor by your verses, which need not the setting off of your music to make them worthy of our best poets."

Mr. Dryden coughed dryly, and looked a trifle vexed that the lines of the unknown so far outshone his, as of a truth they did.

"Very pretty, very pretty, Mr. Domino," said he at last. "I will borrow them for my new play, and put them into the mouth of a callow stripling fresh from school, who thinks women are to be won by lollipops and sweet-meat songs."

"So you shall — so you shall," answered the singer with a grand bow, "though it is a quaint conceit to make a stripling the best speaker in the play."

At this Mr. Dryden looked so black that Mr. Pepys made haste to divert the conversation by saying: "Penelope, my dear, 'tis for you to give us a toast."

"Then," said Penelope, looking down shyly, and then up with a wonderful tremulous sweetness which won all hearts, "it cannot be a merry one; but I will ask you, friends, as you bear me good will, to drink to the health of one who lies this night behind prison bars under sentence of death, but to whom under God, and with the guidance of Captain Bennett in his good ship 'White Lady,' I go with the message of pardon and release.

"I give you *Bryan Fairfax!*"

The toast was drunk most heartily, and scarcely were the goblets drained when the tall stranger, — not he of the lute, but his comrade, — rising, said:

"Good people, I too will give you a toast ere I leave. I ask you to drink the health of the brave maiden who hath come three thousand miles alone in search of this pardon, ay, and braved greater perils than she herself may ever guess to gain it. Stand up and drink the health of Mistress Payne!"

There was somewhat in the stranger's manner which bent all to his will, and without any knowing how it came to pass, his rising was the signal for the company to rise; and though all were burning with curiosity to learn who he was and whence he came, and how he chanced to know so much of the party, none dared question him.

The goblets were set down, having been all drained to the last drop, and there was a general move toward the donning of hats and cloaks and hoods amid much laughter and merriment.

Under cover of the general confusion, the two dominos drew near Penelope. "Your fortune has fallen out even better than I foretold the other evening at Whitehall; — the soothsayer wishes you joy." So spoke the mandolin-player, and moved swiftly out of sight. His companion followed, and bent low to kiss Penelope's hand. As he did so, he slipped upon her wrist an armlet clasped with a true lover's-knot set in diamonds, and in her ear he whispered: " As thou hast been true to thy lover, be true also to thy promise to the King. Pray for him! Perchance to that intercession at the throne of the King of kings he may owe his pardon hereafter."

Scarcely had Penelope had time to take in the words he was speaking ere he had slipped out into the night, whither his companion had gone before. With much mirth and some sadness the rest made their adieux, and so late had they tarried that it was nearly midnight when Mr. Pepys and his niece were set down at their own door in Crutched Friars. Godfrey Kneller had come with them, his homeward way lying with theirs; and when they parted, Penelope thanked him with tears for the service he had done her. Mr. Pepys begged him to come in. The hour being so late, however, he would not; but he told Penelope, smiling, that he was the least bereft of all those she was leaving, since he would still be able to look at the picture of Mistress " Spring," and fancy the original sitting there in the great oak chair beneath the window in his studio. So he spoke his farewell, and Mr.

Pepys and his niece went into the little house in Seething Lane together for the last time.

"Good night, Penelope, and God bless thee!" said her uncle, taking her head between his hands and kissing her on the forehead with much tenderness, wishing, it may be, that Heaven had bestowed on him a daughter who could be to him for life what this maid had been for a few weeks. But Mr. Pepys was a practical man, and his moods of sentiment rarely lasted long.

"Thou art a good girl," he said. "I am loath to part with thee, and I do not grudge thee thy foy, though it cost me two pounds seven shillings (the extra shillings being for the entertainment of the masks). Troth, I would give as much more to discover who they were! People of importance I dare be sworn from their bearing; and when the cloak of the mandolin-player slipped I did catch a glimpse of some huge noble lace at his wrist."

Penelope flushed guiltily, but the secret being none of hers she felt it wrong to say aught of the matter; so hiding her armlet closer beneath her cloak she returned her uncle's good night and ran upstairs to her chamber and sat herself down to write a last entry in her journal. Thus it read:

"Monday night. So will I set it down, though 't were nearer the truth to write it Tuesday morning, for the bellman hath just cried beneath my window, 'Past one o'clock, and a cold, frosty, windy morning.' My candle burns low, and I must make haste to set down the things (many of them too strange almost for belief) that have happed on this, my last night in England. Day will soon break,—a new day leading toward the new world. Thank God, Bryan, it leads me toward thee!"

CHAPTER XIX.

APRIL TWENTY-THIRD.

"One moment in Annihilation's waste,
One moment of the well of life to taste —
The stars are setting, and the caravan
Starts for the dawn of Nothing. Oh, make haste!"

ON the twenty-third day of April, in the year of our Lord sixteen hundred and seventy-seven, the sun rose over the Old Dominion as clear and bright as though, in all the realms his rays shone on, there were no such things as tears or clouded lives or broken human hearts. It was a spring day, and a spring day such as can be found ir Virginia alone. The sky brooded above the earth, the air was a caress, the warm ground thrilled with the quickening of the green things hid in her bosom ready to bourgeon and blossom in a few more days.

Strange paradox! All this sweetness and brightness was but the background of a scene of suffering, and the sad trappings of a humiliating death.

April Twenty-third.

As Bryan Fairfax looked forth from the barred window of his prison in the midst of the ruins of Jamestown, he felt a sudden, bitter pang that Nature should thus, as it were, hold high festival on the day of his death. But to one man in the colony it seemed altogether fitting that the day should rise in unclouded brightness,—for was it not the day of his final triumph and revenge?

Sir William Berkeley had resolved that Bryan Fairfax should hang. He would listen neither to entreaties nor expostulations on that subject. The man who had turned the tide in the field at Gloucester (for that too had come to the Governor's ears), who had secured the safely hidden commission for Bacon, who had beyond a peradventure planned his own taking off (of this he would admit no shadow of doubt),—that man must die. But Fairfax once dead, Berkeley was resolved to play the rôle of father of the people. Nay, he had even prepared a proclamation of general amnesty to be read from the scaffold, so that the remainder of the day following the execution should be given up to popular rejoicing; and if there were those who of late had murmured against the harshness of the government, their voices should be swallowed up in the shouts and acclamations of the crowd.

So carefully had the Governor planned all this, that as the time drew near, he began to feel a nervous dread lest something should go wrong, and his revenge and his pardon alike slip through his fingers. For the last fortnight he had scanned the surface of the river the first thing each morning and the last each evening, dreading lest he should see thereon the broad, square sails of a bark from over seas. Once, indeed, a ship appeared, of such a size that a fear smote him that Penelope Payne might be standing on her deck with the King's pardon held like a white dove in her hand. But the vessel proved to be only a thick-set, round-sterned, tub-like packet from the colony of New Netherland, and Sir William breathed freely once more. For his further consolation the coast had been harassed by heavy storms, which must, as he thought, have beaten back any vessel coming this way, or at least stayed her on her course.

This morning, as he stood upon the bank and saw the broad yellow stream stretching from shore to shore as far as eye could reach, with not so much as a pinnace or a canoe upon its bosom, and the air above so calm that no sail could fill to bear a vessel on, — this old man, unconscious of his blasphemy, lifted up his voice and thanked God aloud that his enemy was delivered into his hand. Nay, the very words of holy writ did he pervert to his evil purpose, saying, " I will tread on him in my anger, and trample him in my fury, and his blood shall be sprinkled upon my garments; for the day of vengeance is in my heart."

So buried was he in his thoughts of blood and vengeance that he heard not the footsteps behind him till he felt a hand laid upon his arm, when, turning, he saw close beside him the tall form and white head of Colonel Payne.

" I am favored, Sir William, to find you here, for I was about to seek you at your house."

" A visit from Colonel Payne is alway an honor," replied Berkeley; but there was little heart in the words.

A chill had fallen of late betwixt these two men who had been of old such dear friends; and when a blight once falls on friendship, there is no shower save tears of contrition that can revive it.

" It was not a visit of ceremony, but on official business," said Colonel Payne. " I have already in vain besought you for the sake of your own honor, as well as in the name of mercy, to delay the sentence of this unfortunate young man, Bryan Fairfax, till the coming in of the ship, which may be even now upon the ocean, bearing the King's pardon."

" I do appreciate your zeal in his behalf, and I

might be moved to grant your petition, and wish you joy of a future son-in-law with the smell o' James City jail on his garments; but I have a duty to the State."

Colonel Payne reddened with anger at the first words; but as he looked on the Governor's livid face distorted with hatred and malice, and all the evil passions that spring up in their train, he felt a great overwhelming pity for this man who had once stood at the parting of the ways, his nature rich in qualities both good and bad, and who had deliberately turned away from his better nature and thrown the reins upon the neck of his baser passions, which were now in a mad gallop none could check. To reason with him was as futile as to argue with a madman. But Colonel Payne said quietly: "I can conceive no duty to the State which waits not upon the King's will, and methinks this obstinacy smacks more of private vengeance than of care for the common weal."

The truth of the accusation made it unbearable. Berkeley writhed as if a probe had been turned in a wound. "Colonel Payne!" he cried in fury, "an 't were not for our old-time friendship I 'd have you clapped into the prison along side of Bryan Fairfax for such words to the Governor of the colony."

April Twenty-third.

"No doubt," answered Payne, coldly. "It were quite of a piece with your conduct, and would match well. So far ye have carried all with a high hand, but beware! The King is the father of his people, and they have cried aloud to him of thy cruelty!"

"So," snarled Berkeley, "that was thy daughter's errand, to stir up anger against me as well as to procure a pardon for her precious lover! I am glad to know it, and I will take care to make her home-coming all it should be. Know, Theophilus Payne, that were I to set sail for England this day, I would stay the ship till I had seen Bryan Fairfax hanged."

"Then," said Payne, "there is no more to be said. I will stand by Fairfax on the scaffold as though he were mine own son, as for my dear daughter's sake I do verily count him. For you, your deeds be upon your head, and never, so help me God, will I speak to you or take you by the hand so long as Virginia shall hold us both."

The long roll of the drum broke in upon the words, and Colonel Payne's face grew ashen white as he saw the prison door open and Bryan Fairfax come forth, guarded before and behind by two stout halberdiers.

The four months in prison had left their traces. Fairfax had entered the jail a youth, — he emerged a man. The deep furrows between the eyes had been drawn by the hand of grief; yet the head with its weight of fair hair was lifted as haughtily as of old. Neither to the right nor the left did he turn as he marched up the straggling village street where half a year since he had ridden a conqueror, now surrounded by a hooting mob.

"'T is pity your General is na with you to see the ruins o' the houses ye laid in ashes last fall," cried one in his ear.

"Ay," added a smoother tone on the other side; "and a pity Mistress Payne cannot take in this scene from her ship. Could I have had my say, I would have built the scaffold like a lighthouse tower, and set it where it might be as a beacon to in-coming vessels."

The color rose to the pale cheek of Fairfax, and his hands, bound with rope as they were, fumbled nervously for his sword. But he only lifted his head the higher and marched forward with firm tread and steady eye.

Ere he had gone another rod, the place on his right was taken by Colonel Payne.

"Courage, my lad!" quoth he. "I have watchers posted on the river bank. We have three hours yet, and if the ship heave in sight, Berkeley *dare* not proceed."

April Twenty-third.

"How say you, Colonel Payne?" spoke Arthur Thorn from the other side. "'*Dare not*' are harsh words to be used anent an old soldier, and sure no man ever deserved it less. I will see to it that your speech reaches His Excellency."

"Say what you like," answered the Colonel. "'T were as hard to increase the Governor's malignity as your poisonous sycophancy."

"Excellent words!" quoth Thorn, his tawny face mottling like the skin of a snake. "Excellent words, — treason and libel all in one. I will find my way to Governor Berkeley with them, and that without loss of time." With this he took his leave, yet for some time hovered near, as loath even for a moment to lose sight of his victim.

"Colonel Payne," said Fairfax when Thorn had gone, his face for the first time relaxing from its stony composure, "tell Penelope that I died as a soldier should, and that on the very scaffold, looking death in the face, the thought of her love made me a proud and happy man."

The Colonel turned away. There was that in his throat which made it impossible to utter speech. In silence, keeping step as to a funeral march, they went on together, shoulder to shoulder. Oh, what joy and comfort it brought afterward to the heart of Penelope Payne to remember that her father and her lover were thus united to the very end!

As they drew near the foot of the scaffold the crowd, attracted more by curiosity than hatred, grew thicker. A little lad stepped out from those who lined the road, and held forth toward Fairfax a bunch of gay wild-flowers gripped tight in his tiny chubby fist; then as he saw the prisoner's hands bound tight behind him he cried, "Poor man! thou canst not hold the flowers I did gather for thee."

"Nay, little one," answered Fairfax with a smile sadder than tears, "no more flowers for me in this world; but I thank thee none the less for thy kind intention." Small as was the act, it shed a glow over Fairfax's downcast heart and with its last beat came a picture of that childish hand outstretched with its bunch of flowers. It was strange how now in his great stress of mind his eye noted every blossom and singled out the white violet, the wood anemone, and the hanging crimson bell of the columbine.

It was nine o'clock, and the sun already waxing hot, when Bryan Fairfax took his stand upon the scaffold, the cruel rope about his neck, that he might experience for three mortal hours the full foretaste of the death agony.

April Twenty-third.

In full sight from the scaffold, in the centre of the village green, stood the dial; and from where he stood Fairfax could watch the shadow creep along, and to him it was like the shadow of death cast by the sun of eternity. Strange to say, he had no wish to stay it, but would fain have hastened it rather in a kind of mad impatience to be done with it all and learn the worst that life (or death) had in store for him. Yet one thought ran under and through all his feelings. "Penelope! Poor Penelope!"

The shadow on the dial marked ten.

A strange, trancelike feeling had stolen over him. He seemed to be but one of the crowd around the scaffold, and to see himself as a stranger standing there uplifted in ignominy. He listened then with scarce a thrill of emotion to the murmurs of sympathy which ran through the throng of bystanders, mostly women.

"How handsome he is!"

"And so young!"

"Ay, and his poor sweetheart gone to fetch the King's pardon. Poor thing, she'll go mad when she finds she is come too late, and maybe kill herself."

"Then Berkeley will have the blood of two on his head, for 'tis sheer murder."

"The blood of two! Say rather of two hundred,—and none knows whose turn will come next. I would the King were here to see what things be done in his name."

To all this Fairfax listened as calmly as though he had no interest of special moment in the discourse,—nay, all his senses seemed quickened beyond the natural. He noted the dignitaries on the platform,—that Sir John Berry wore a new sword-belt, that Philip Ludwell had grown a mustachio, and that Governor Berkeley's eyes were shot with blood, which was not so aforetime.

The shadow on the dial marked eleven.

Colonel Payne paced up and down like a caged lion, his eye fixed in turn upon the boat in the river and the man on the shore, watching, watching for the red flag which was to be the signal of an approaching vessel. Would it never come! Ah, what bitter irony should it come but one hour too late! Despair had settled black on Payne's soul; yet still he sought to cheer the other, bidding him be of good courage, for while there was life there was hope. But like a running comment of mockery on his words were the preparations going on around, the hangman making ready and testing the strength of the beam.

Now there crept over Fairfax a sharp, pricking

April Twenty-third.

sense that this was indeed the last of earth. He strove to give up his heart wholly to God, and to shut out all thoughts and affections of this world; but spite of his intensest effort God seemed shadowy, strange, and far away, and every pulsation of his being throbbed with one word, one thought: "Penelope! Penelope! Penelope!"

The shadow on the dial marked the half hour.

The moments slid away. A silence fell on the crowd like the calm which goes before a storm. The air was electric with feeling. —

"Hark!"

"Heard ye aught?"

"Ay, of a truth, methought I caught the sound of flying hoofs on yonder bridge."

"See, see, — 't is a woman who rides!"

"What if 't were — "

"Nay! Nay! It could na be."

"Yea, I swear, 't is she!"

While these breathless whispers were running from mouth to mouth in the crowd, Bryan Fairfax stood with fixed and glassy eyes upon the scaffold. So absorbed was his soul in the thought of Penelope that it was scarcely with surprise that his mind conjured up the vision of her form on horseback as he had seen her that day of their ride to this very spot; but now she was flying like some wild sister of the wind up the street, and her horse was trembling, flecked with foam and with wide distended nostrils. Such apparitions he had heard did oftentimes arise before the eyes of those about to die. But what struck him as most strange was the fact that the hangman paused in his ghastly work, and the very crowd around his feet seemed to share his delusion, for a mighty cheer arose from beneath him, — a cheer which shook the platform on which with staring eyes and open mouth and swelling veins stood the Governor.

"Hurrah!" shouted the crowd.

"Penelope!"

"Penelope Payne!"

Yes, it was she. Finding the ship becalmed upon the lower river, she had taken horse, and outstripping those who rode with her, she had reached the fatal spot in time; but with not one moment to spare. Flinging herself from the horse, which already swayed this way and that, ready to sink upon its spent knees, she waved a white packet above her head, and rushing up the rude steps of the platform fell on her knees before the Governor, crying: "The King's pardon! In time, thank God!"

Berkeley turned a terrible ashen gray; then pointing his rigid arm to the shadow on the dial which marked three minutes after twelve he gasped: "Nay, by God, 't is *not* in time. Bid the hangman do his office!"

"Never!" shouted the crowd, suddenly grown a menacing mob.

"The King's pardon must be respected, Your Excellency," said Sir John Berry, courteously but firmly.

Berkeley stamped with fury. "It came too late, I say. But for the gaping and gazing of the hangman the sentence would have been already executed when this wench arrived. If need be, my own hands shall make fast the rope. I am Governor of this province, and I *will* be obeyed."

With trembling hands Penelope tore open the breast of her gown, and, drawing forth a paper sealed with the royal seal, she thrust it into Sir John Berry's hands, crying out, "Lose not an instant, — read! read!"

The Governor himself paused and turned, spellbound by the girl's voice, and the crowd waited in the hush born of intense excitement. Sir John glanced hastily, with ever-growing amazement, at the paper, and then, advancing to the edge of the platform, he said aloud so that all could hear: "I do hold in my hand a communication from our sovereign Lord the King. Under any circumstances but the extraordinary ones now existing, I should deem it most unfitting to make it public till it had been first communicated to him whom it doth most concern; but in view of the great issue at stake, I do accept the heavy responsibility of making it here known to the people of Virginia."

Having so said, amid a hush still as death he spread out the sheet and read:

To Sir John Berry, Knight:

TRUSTY AND WELL-BELOVED,— We greet you well. Whereas it hath come to our knowledge that affairs in our province of Virginia are gone sadly awry, it is our will that all be investigated and thoroughly considered, and to this end we command Sir William Berkeley, our trusty vice-regent, to return at once to England, and we do hereby order and decree that from the moment this paper is placed in your hands, the powers and privileges of Governor of the province be lodged and vested in you until such time as the Lieutenant-Governor, Sir Herbert Jeffreys, can be proclaimed, in due form of law, Governor in place of Sir William Berkeley. And for the instant and full performance of these our commands we rely upon your well-approved loyalty.

CHARLES R.

Stillness deep as death fell on the multitude. Then Sir John said solemnly:

"As my first official act, in the King's name, I bid yonder hangman remove the rope from about the neck of Bryan Fairfax, and I declare the prisoner pardoned."

The scene which followed is beyond the power of my poor pen to set down. It was as though in the setting free of this one man the whole colony felt itself shaking off the yoke of an intolerable tyranny. Men kissed and hugged each other like women. Women wept like infants, and children shouted as lustily as men. Two alone in that great throng stood as if dazed, unable to comprehend the event. Fairfax and Berkeley faced each other, stiff and mute as statues. A moment only this mutual gaze lasted, for the feeling was too tense for long endurance. At the end of two minutes the Governor was seen to sway to and fro, and he would have fallen but for Sir John Berry, who caught him, and laying him back in his chair called for some one to fetch water, which broke the spell which had fallen on the crowd and diverted their gaze from this group upon the platform.

"My God, — it cannot be!" were the first words Berkeley uttered as he came to himself. Then, as if the whole weight of his misfortune fell on him at once, he gave a mighty cry: "Put not thy trust in princes. Ah, Strafford, t' was well said!"

"Nay, Your Excellency," said Ludwell, placing his arm over his shoulder, "lay not the matter so to heart! Mayhap the King doth but desire to make inquiry into the matter, and hath sent for thee to inform him further touching the business. Didst thou not mark how he spake of thee as his trusty servant? Another Spring may see thee seated firmer in power than ever."

"Think not to prop me thus with hopes as false as princes' favor," answered Berkeley, rising and shaking off the friendly hand. "I am undone. All my years of faithful service count for naught against the word of this prating pink and white fool, who doubtless hath purchased my ruin with her own."

"*Thou liest!*"

The words came forth like cannon-shot from the lips of Colonel Payne, who had stood by till now silent and stunned with the tide of feeling which engulfed him.

Berkeley turned, his face one crimson fury, and would have rushed upon the speaker; but Ludwell and Beverley threw themselves between the two men.

"Stay thy hand for a time," whispered Ludwell in Berkeley's ear. "Give thine enemies no further handle for the tool of their revenge. Come away home with me!"

"Ay, come," said Beverley, taking him gently by the other arm.

April Twenty-third.

The crowd parted to make room for the three men, and they passed between the lines amid a hush unbroken by a single cheer. It was hard but it was just. Berkeley had sown the wind, it was meet that he should reap the whirlwind. He had given up to evil passions a nature once swayed by generous emotions. Under that baleful shadow, zeal had turned to bigotry, firmness to obstinacy, authority to tyranny, martial ardor to thirst for blood, and the world sadly marked one more soul lost through the perversion of its good qualities. Thus it came about that as the Governor passed along his valley of humiliation none bade him "God speed!" none breathed a sigh of sympathy. He who had proved himself pitiless now could look for no pity.

> "The Sons of wrath have perished by the blow
> Themselves had aimed at others long ago."

One man only grieved, — ay, grieved as deeply and gnawed his very heart out as uselessly as the Governor himself in his impotent rage over a frustrated purpose and a broken vengeance. Arthur Thorn stood gazing with black, furtive, maddened eyes at Fairfax, and his hand played nervously about the hilt of his sword. His manner did but too clearly shadow forth the murderous thoughts which lurked in his soul, and one who noted both them and him said scornfully:

"'T is of no use, young man. Your game is escaped. An ye would not find Fairfax's rope around your own neck, and not for form's sake this time, nor to be shaken off by whimpering for pardon, I do counsel you to take yourself out of this colony along with your protector."

"Ay," said another, "get ye gone with the Governor. 'T is in part to your sneaking support that he owes his present plight."

"Out of town with him to the tune of the rogue's march!" cried a third.

So excited was the crowd becoming that Thorn thought it prudent to test its temper no longer; but leaping on his horse, vanished in the direction of Green Spring.

As he was never heard of more in the Old Dominion, it was suspected that he lay in hiding till the setting sail of the Governor, which came to pass on the twenty-seventh of April, and departed with him.

It was a good riddance for the colony.

And what of Bryan Fairfax? Who will dare attempt to describe the feelings of a man, recalled thus in an instant from an ignominious death to love and life and all that makes life dear?

April Twenty-third.

Those who saw him that day were wont to tell, for years after, the story of his look as he stood there upon the scaffold as upon a throne, by his side the maiden who had dared and suffered so much for his sake. Thus they stood together, oblivious of all the world,—she gazing up through her tears, he (his bonds having been severed by the knife of Colonel Payne) clasping her closer, ever closer, to his heart.

"Ah, Penelope," he whispered, "that song of thine was a true prophecy. Love *has* found out the way!"

THE END.

www.ingramcontent.com/pod-product-compliance
Lightning Source LLC
Chambersburg PA
CBHW030731230426
43667CB00007B/670